This book belongs to:

ANNETTE STEDTLER

our nice aunt and
cousin

Love

Alexandra &
Choruka

Berlin 18.11.95

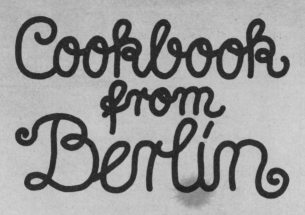

Cookbook from Berlin

Collected, recorded, and tested by
Fritz Becker

published by
Wolfgang Hölker

ISBN: 3-88117-446-X

© 1988 Verlag Wolfgang Hölker,
Martinistrasse 2, D-4400 Münster
Translation: Jacqueline Jeffers
All rights reserved
Printed in West-Germany by
Druckhaus Cramer, Greven

Table of Contents

fig. 1 **A Gastronomic Stroll through Old Berlin** 8–27

fig. 2 **Drinks** 28–33

fig. 3 **Soups** 34–41

fig. 4 **Traditional, simple Dishes** 42–47

fig. 5 **Vegetables** 48–55

fig. 6 **Egg Dishes** 56–61

fig. 7 **Fish Dishes** 62–73

fig. 8 **Meat and Poultry Dishes** 74–99

fig. 9 **Cold Dishes** 100–109

fig. 10 **Sweets and Pastries** 110–121

fig. 11 **Index** 122–127

Metric Conversion chart 127

All recipes serve 4 people.

Foreword

In recording these traditional Prussian recipes, the author has also recorded his own experiences. I got to know him in my own restaurant, "Genueser Schiff," where, as my chef, he introduced arithmetic, Prussian frugality, and the most delicious menus. The guests' table conversation thus frequently centered around the good food.

Prussian recipes have long since found their way into international cuisine. For lovers of local cuisine, may this book serve as a guide to finding it in its authentic form in Berlin.

Gabriele Brandt –
– Gräfin Waldersee

Joh. Haenlehel Berlin

Court kitchen at the Berlin City Palace

Berliners have always believed that a good roasted goose is a gift from God.

Thus there is no lack of early handbooks on the art of real Berlin cooking in Brandenburg. There was even an early guide to proper nutrition by someone named Elsholtz, or the Brandenburg cookbook inspired by an academic authority from Helmstedt named Professor H. Conring. Not to forget the cookbook "Wie man in Berlin z. Zt. der Königin Luise kochte," describing the style of cooking during the era of Queen Luise, authored by Jenny Sommerfeldt, née Fontane, and Elise Weber, née Fontané, both related to our "prince among poets," Theodor Fontane.

Both ladies based their work on the recipe collection of Mrs. Auguste Fontane, née Werner, the third wife of Pierre Barthélemy Fontane, Secretary of the Cabinet of Queen Luise.

Considering the costliness of the ingredients of many of these recipes, it follows that they were intended only for ladies of the upper class, who had only to give orders and sit at the table, without concerning themselves with the actual preparation of meals.

Thus it is not surprising that the court doctor, Elsholtz, describes graphically such exotic dishes as Indian Bird's Nest soup. In his letters, the writer Heinrich Heine later describes delicacies prepared by the then-renowned court restaurateur, Jagor. "Ye Gods, how easily I could make you forget ambrosia by describing the mountain of sweets there. Aphrodite, have you experienced a sweet meringue?"

Let us continue our stroll through old Berlin!

The chronicles record a delightful new cookbook by a Mrs. Anna Wecker which was published in 1598 in Amberg.

This cookbook was used in the household of the famous Commissioner Fritze, who was in the service of the prince. He lived on Poststrasse, where he died in 1630.

In 1607, Mrs. Wecker's cookbook was still in the possession of Princess Elisabeth in Crossen. Anna Wecker was the widow of Dr. Johann Jacob Wecker, who was the actual author of the cookbook.

Royal invoices dating back to the 17th century clearly reflect that Bohemian cuisine set the tone at the time. In 1606, the Prince had his cook, Hansen, trained in Prague. Ten years later, Prince Johannes Sigismund awarded his personal cook, Master Zichel, with an annuity in appreciation for his services.

Other history sources reveal that the ruling Minister Count Schwarzenberg, also known for his good taste in clothes, brought back a cook from France. In 1634, this cook prepared a few meals for the Prince for which he received 25 gold pieces.

Cooks received such handsome remuneration that the royal chef Hans Bentorate was even in a position to lend a young, indebted aristocrat the considerable amount of 100 gold pieces.

Frederick the Great's head chefs enjoyed high social standing. The roasting chef, Mecho, was occasionally even permitted to act as escort to the Queen Mother. In a newsletter dated February 25, 1754, a notice describes a sword lost between Langer Brücke and Brüderstrasse, and that the honest finder should deliver it to Mr. Mecho. He had lost it while on a stroll.

The longtime chef of Frederick the Great, Noël, also known as "Newton of the soup pot," enjoyed special privileges with the monarch. Chodowieki captured Noël in a diorama that depicted him under an umbrella at a masked ball at Frederick's court.

Frederick Wilhelm II was also a gourmet. His chief chef Rieck had a habit of parading around in a uniform. According to a report by the Minister of Security, Finance, and Justice, von Woellner, the honorable magistrate also made use of Rieck's culinary services.

In 1797, cod – then considered a delicacy – was first served at a Charlottenburg wedding. Previously, during the reign of Frederick II and Frederick Wilhelm I, cod was considered unfit for a royal banquet. At the same time, pike perch was less popular, a definite reflection of the abundance of fish in the still-clear surrounding waters. The first pike perch recipe appeared in 1733 and called for a mustard broth. A wigmaker and his sergeant friend invented the recipe, a forerunner to the dish known as Cod with Mustard Butter. Later, in 1822, the restaurateur Jagor formally introduced this dish. It is still popular today. Turbot then appeared as a new palate-pleaser in Berlin.

11

Brillat-Savarin dedicates a whole chapter to this fish in his "Physiology of Taste." Old menus reveal that another noble fish, sole, was the next fish to emerge as the culinary highlight.

The Baking Trade in Berlin

Guild signs displayed outside Hamburg's bakeries showed rolls or baker's paddles. Berlin, however, paid tribute to the pretzel. This has remained the traditional symbol of the baker's guild in Berlin and the surrounding area. It appeared for the first time in the town of Havelberg in 1527. The custom of eating pretzels ("Brezel") apparently had early christian origins. It was not an everyday pastry, but one that was eaten especially on holidays. The name "Brezel" stems from the Middle Ages prefix of the Latin word "Brachiola." It is presumed to have been a devotional food depicting the crossed arms of a disciple. The spiritual connection with the pretzel is still apparent in church today, during holy holidays, fasting periods, and funeral services.

In the 12th century, nuns in "hortus deliciarum" served pretzels as dessert following the fish, as compensation for forbidden pleasures.

In 1725, during the period from Ash Wednesday to March 14, the Protestant Queen Sophie Dorothee had a box of butter and sweet pretzels delivered to her in Potsdam every day. In a letter dated January 9, 1824, to Zelter, Goethe wrote that his mother had forgotten to indicate in her last will and testament the size of pretzels to be served with the wine to the mourners. At the time, it was customary in the city of Frankfurt for pallbearers to receive half a pretzel before the funeral, and a whole one afterwards.

In his travel report of 1781, Johann Bernouilli from the Uckermark reported a ban on pretzel baking, intended to save wood. According to the annual invoice of 1716/17, the children at the orphanage in the town of Lindow near Ruppin received pretzels for Christmas. Pursuant to a church invoice dated 1737 from Tempelfelde, pretzels were handed out initially on Maundy Thursday and later on Good Friday.

In the town of Oderberg, pretzels were distributed to the Town Hall auditorium for passed exams. At the church choir in the town Kirchhaim in Niederlausitz it was customary as of 1595 to serve "choir pretzels" with warm beer on the occasion of their annual meeting festivities.

At the sailors' Mardi Gras in the town of Rathen, a "Brezelmann" presided in a robe.

The annals tell of a "pretzel lady" from Lenzen, who left a legacy for poor children. Her tombstone in the local churchyard is worth seeing. In 1735, the Berlin bakers' guild voted to temporarily give permission to a poor master baker to bake pretzels to regain financial footing.

In time, many different types of pretzels evolved. A certain woman from the town of Spandau named Ricke gained fame because she loudly hawked her cinnamon pretzels in front of the Spandau Castle. In 1819, the royal Prussian "Hofküchenmeister," Samentzky, described several types of pretzels in his "Lehrbuch der Kochkunst" (a guide to the art of cooking), including "Englische Blätterbrezeln, Bärm-Bräzeln à l'Allemande, Hanauer, Hannöver'sche Bräzeln." In a newspaper advertisement dated January 31, 1735, a Mrs. Storbeck offered almond pretzels for sale. On March 6, 1754, the pastry baker Töppen offered Bremer pretzels for 6 pfennigs in the cellar of the house of Mr. Petitot. On November 7, 1794, master baker Keyser had Nurenberg pretzels for sale. Goullon, personal cook to the Saxonian Duke in Weimar, October 22, 1818, tells of a "pretzel dance" at a mill on the Spree River behind the town of Moabit. The custom of pretzel dances is portrayed in an engraving by Chodowiecki called "Wallfahrt nach Französisch Buchholz."

Prince Louis Ferndinand's "Hofmeister" Knoblauch revealed his recipe for small butter pretzels in his cookbook from 1829.

In the middle of the 18th century, a burgher by the name of Steffen introduced himself as a pretzel baker and sold his fresh pretzels on the Mühlendamm underneath the apartment of the Chief Mill Inspector in Mrs. Benezles' store.

Wars, inflation, and other influences eventually brought the pretzel custom to an end.

Pâté baking emerged as a new trade in the 16th century. This is recorded in the annals of the city of Cologne. In Berlin, similar entries are recorded in 1603 and 1652.

In 1578, Hiobst Kettelin was the royal pastry chef. In 1601, Kettelin, among others, received a New Year's gratification of 20 gold pieces and is pronounced "Mundkoch" (personal cook to the King).

In 1735, an English pastry cook arrives, and in March 1750 the pastry cook Grey. In 1742, Ambrosius Haude published a new booklet for the price of 4 pennies called "Englischer Koch nebst einem Küchenzettel auf vornehme Tafeln wo die Rezepturen für Pastete nachzulesen sind." It should be mentioned here that eel pâté was a favorite of Frederick the Great.

Grey also called himself a restaurateur. On the Breite Strasse in the Drewitz house, he operated a coffee shop with billiard tables. It was said that he would continue catering weddings and other occasions, as well as serve lunch and dinner specials. His catering services also included fine wines. It is hereby apparent that making pâtés was not considered a special profession, but rather as part of a first-class culinary repertoire.

In 1771, the former royal cook Gebhard moved from the restaurant "9 Churfürsten" in the Scharrenstrasse to the restaurant "Weisser Schwan" in the Jüdenstrasse. His pâtés were among the delicacies ordered by distinguished patrons.

In 1498, pâté was considered the ne plus ultra in the art of cooking. It was served for the first time by the Lord Mayor of the city of Frankfurt/Oder as the high point of a banquet for Frederick Wilhelm I, known to be connoisseur of good food such as oysters, caviar, truffles, larks, and pheasants. In those days, Berlin appeared deserted around noontime. Only the domestics scurried about, carrying their pâté baskets.

This rich dish was rather unhealthy, and it is reported that physicians were very much in demand. Stomach brushes were also

14

offered. In 1713, a paper ("Chronik Skandaleuse") reported of the death of a member of the "Round Table of Sanssouci" following an elaborate dinner at the residence of the envoy, Tyrconel. The victim, a doctor, succumbed to a truffle pâté.

Frederick used to send such pâtés to his friend, the Canon to Brandenburg. Dr. Zimmermann, Frederick's personal physician, noted in his published reports that pâtés contributed considerably to the worsening of his patient's condition. Zimmermann is referring specifically to the aforementioned eel pâté. Vension or other meat pâtés as served at Dr. Sprögel's residence on Spandauer Strasse were easier on the stomach.

In July, 1742, the chronicles report of a wedding feast at a vicarage in Charlottenburg, where grouse pâté was served and kept on the table as a centerpiece until the third course.

In 1779, Georg Förster wrote a detailed letter to Jakobi describing the gluttony and debauchery in Berlin. By 1638, under Frederick Wilhelm, the finances of the state were in such poor condition that the royal kitchen had to borrow 15 gold pieces from the Magistrate. In 1817, Prince Pückler Muskau ordered the first pâté de foie gras de canard from Toulouse and sent one to his fiancée. On his menu of May, 1822, the royal restaurateur Jagor offered only cold goose liver pâté and "small pâtés" as served by Abraham Bosses in the petit pâtissier.

In an advertisement dated April 26, 1793, the restaurateur Pankow offered small pâtés, approximately one dozen per tray. The members of the Magistrate ate these during their official visits to court hearings in the surrounding area. Decades later common burghers were also able to enjoy these delicacies with evening music at better restaurants, where hosts usually served chicken pâté. The cook Kuhnert served these pâtés in August of 1810 in the Louisen-Kirchgasse, the cook Dietrich in August of 1817 in the Tiergarten. One hundred years earlier, in 1723, the Brandenburger Cookbook offered the aristocracy recipes for snail and artichoke pâtés, oyster pâtés, lark pâtés, and 74 other types. In 1733, a pastry shop in Sorau had exactly 103 clay pâté molds and 153 tin pâté rings at their disposal.

Fruit and Other Exotic Dishes in Old Berlin

In spite of the transportation difficulties involved, Prince Joachim II loved oysters. In Berlin they were called Oéstrichen! According the chamber records from 1616, a courier from Lüneburg transported 3600 of these shellfish as far as Grimnitz for a fee of 32 gold and 17 silver pieces. The next couriers mentioned are Christian Weiler, 1624, and Walter Rowe, a musician. In 1613 and 1632, two small pots of oysters are sent to a friendly duchy in Dresden. Improved German-Russian relations following the independence wars resulted in the availability of genuine Russian caviar at an Italian store owned by Sala Tarone near the "Schleusenbrücke."

Theodor Fontane made Russian caviar famous in 1784.

A Berlin gazette reported, "The Russian merchant A. Utschakoff from Moscow has arrived with good, fresh caviar" (March 8, 1790, and previously on January 22, 1790). In consideration of the wealthy Russian clientele, caviar is also served in the Hôtel de Russie. Goethe stayed in this hotel in 1778.

Wilhelm v. Humboldt sent 2 pots of caviar to Goethe in Weimar in 1797, and eel sometime thereafter.

The first cranberries arrived in Berlin around this time. The merchant Hünefeld brings them as preserves on October 6, 1786. They are described as a healthy delicacy and popular accompaniment for many meat dishes. In 1577, Rochus Lynar, a fortress builder, sent an exotic fruit basket ("de beaux citrons et pommes d'adam et grenades") to the wife of the Administrator and later Prince of the town of Halle, Friedrich. The recipient thanked him "avec grand plaisir," as exotic fruit was a rarity.

Lynar's fruit basket contained sweet pomegranates (also known as portogallo), lemons and limes, and grapefuit. The sweet pomegranate was also known as "orange de chine" because of its Chinese origin. In 1768 it was called "sinasapple" and then "apple de sine." Three hundred years after reaching Berlin, oranges cost 2 gold pieces and 18 pennies per six dozen. Since 1821, a thaler (gold piece) had been worth 30 silver pieces at 12 pfennigs each. Oranges came to 1 groschen, 1 pfennig apiece. Market women at the Spittel market charged 10 groschen for 3 oranges. In 1822, the restaurateur Jagor charged 3 groschen per orange. In the 17th century, exotic fruit was considered a necessary luxury at the Brandenburg court. Royal invoices show that in 1616 in Leipzig, lemons were purchased and used to garnish head of wild boar and goose. Lemons were highly appreciated as a refreshment while traveling. The royal pharmacist was responsible for their availability.

In 1614 and 1618 the Kurfürst made his own bulk purchases. He paid 13 thaler, 8 groschen, and 6 pfennigs for 400 lemons. In 1745, 19 thaler, 5 groschen, and 6 pfennigs were paid from Frederick the Great's private account for a crate of 412 lemons, while fifteen years earlier, during his sojourn in Küstrin, he craved a taste of lemon.

Tapestries of Pesne hanging in the Charlottenburg Castle illustrate the value of oranges and lemons. The lemon basket advanced to the plat de ménage and became a part of every respectable table decoration. The annals of 1700, 1670, and 1696 report of the arrival of the first lemon merchants in Berlin. A woman called "schwarze Citronenliese" is mentioned. In the middle of the 18th century, the first "Limonadiers" appeared, selling lemonade by the barrel and in bottles. In 1797, Professor J. S. Halle revealed a recipe for making lemon powder with an authentic lemon taste. This was the first step toward the food industry of the 19th century and the eventual production of powdered milk.

The lemon even had its place at funeral services in Berlin-Brandenburg. The regulations for the handling of corpses in the town of Prenzlau of March 18, 1773, state the following: "The sexton shall receive, in addition a gold piece, a lemon, which may be exchanged for money in the case of the burial of a nobleman." In 1837, the person leading the funeral procession carried the yellow fruit in one hand.

Luise-Henriette of the House of Orange incorporated the fruit in her crest and heraldry.

A Pierre Cuny is reported as the first grower of cherries. In May, 1735, he placed an advertisement in the local paper announcing an abundance of fully ripe May cherries for sale at a low price. Frederick the Great already had developed a great preference for cherries during his stay in Rheinsberg. The first cherries cost 4 groschen apiece. Cuny's January 5, 1745 invoice to Frederick's account refers to a credit of 193 Reichsthaler from the previous year. In 1748, competitors begin to appear, including a man named Christian Schultze who arrived in Berlin on April 21 with 12 apricots at a price of 2 thaler 18 groschen. He was commissioned to start a cherry orchard at Sanssouci.

On March 5, 1686, an edict was issued to the vicars stating that they were to perform no marriages unless the groom – bachelor or widower – could present a notarized paper to his superior that he had planted at least 6 fruit trees and 6 young oak trees. Should the wedding take place during the winter months, he would have to put down a deposit until the spring, not to be returned until he had presented proof of completion of the requirement.

This story should come to mind whenever there is talk of the tree blossoms and fruit wines in Werder near Potsdam.

Around 1750, Frederick the Great generously decreed that the first potato tubers were to be distributed amongst the Prussian for planting. This was done with great fanfare in front of town halls. The initial results were disasterous. According to the farmers, even dogs refused to eat those "things." The most common belief was that they would grow into trees and could then be shaken off like plums or apples. Some stuck them into the ground individually. Others thought they were being clever and buried them all in one pile, which made them grow into a thicket. Frederick instructed his clerks and overseers to conduct a strict "potato watch." Field instructers were sent out, the royal donation was increased in the following year, and only then was the endeavor successful. In 1785, the first potato fields appeared in the Prussian territories. Famines were now a thing of the past. The potato tubers were also known as Toffeln or Töffelen.

Another sweet fruit then became fashionable in Sanssouci – pineapple. The merchant Caspar Bose had pineapples planted in his garden in Leipzig as early as 1685. Receipts from Frederick the Great's private account dated 1747 indicate that he bought pineapples from Glatz. In 1750, the gardener Bartsch in Oranienburg began experimenting with this exotic fruit. Frederick Nicolai spent his later years growing pineapples, which was quite a lucrative hobby. In July of 1797 he received 4 thaler, 20 groschen for 4 pineapples. In 1810, pineapples were offered in flower pots as Christmas gifts for children.

In 1804, Nicolai increased his stock by 100 plants, and in 1809 by 250 plants. After his death the property was maintained, and according to entries in the annals of 1812, went to a privy councillor named Eichmann.

Nicolai's father was the well-known bookseller Christian Gottlieb, who published the booklet "Des Magens Verteidigung der Edlen Austern." The Nicolai bookstore still exists in Berlin. The inventor of the Fürst-Pückler-Bombe (a dessert) also bought his pineapple plant supply in Potsdam. In 1817, he bought 450 one-to-three-year-old plants from the royal gardener Bleichert, to be planted by Muskau on a sandy island next to potatoes and pine trees. His contemporary, Dorothea Schlegel, suggested in her letters that it was inappropriate and useless to plant pineapples where Brandenburg turnips should be planted. Fürst Pückler grew them anyway. His goal was 2000 to 3000 plants annually, and he intended to sell them in Berlin. In 1820, he sent pineapples to his friend Staegemann, and in 1830 to Rahel Varnhagen. Goethe also mentioned this delicacy. In the year of his death, the pastry shop Linden, on the corner of Neustädtische Kirchstrasse, was already selling jelly doughnuts with pineapple filling, which previously had been the exclusive privilege of the wealthy.

Eating and Drinking Customs in Old Berlin

Few Berliners know the origin of the name "Eisbein." The name of this popular dish, served especially during the winter months, originated in the vicinity of the old Görlitz train station. It is related neither to cold weather nor to cold feet. People used to make ice-skate blades for children from pigs' shin bones, which were tied to the shoes. This contraption was called "Eisbein" by the locals. The Casseler Kotelett known throughout Germany was not invented in the city of Kassel, but by a Berlin butcher named Cassel, whose shop was located on Potsdamer Strasse 15.

Jagdwurst used to be called Kaiser-Jagdwurst. The Kaiser is no longer, but Jagdwurst has survived. It is reported that Bockwurst was first sold at the Hackeschen Market. The Butcher's Guild of Berlin claims that Bockwurst first appeared around the Görlitz train station in 1889. An innkeeper on Skalitzer Strasse named Richard Scholtz used to serve Bockbeer to a group of students. He wanted to offer them something special, so he went to a butcher by the name of Löwenthal and bought some of his specialty sausages. After midnight, Scholtz brought out these warm, tasty sausages, which the happy students declared to be the ideal partner for Bockbeer. Henceforth the innkepper was known as "Bockwurst-Scholtz," and the sausage became one of the most popular items on the menu. Berlin is unimaginable without its sausage vendors. Berliners eat their sausages as quick snacks either with potato salad or rolls. During the 1948/49 blockade, Berlin sorely missed the little sausages.

Aschinger, a restaurant chain decorated in the blue and white state colors of Bavaria, initiated the sausage evolution in Berlin, beginning with Aschinger's "Bierwurst" and gratis rolls. As told to me by one of its managers, Aschinger sees itself as a kind of welfare institution, especially toward the end of the month, because nowhere else can you stand at a counter and eat a bowl of puréed peas with gratis rolls.

On our browse through old Berlin, the following typical dishes should not be forgotten: Mutton ribs with green beans; Bratwurst in beer sauce with mashed potatoes (Stolzer Heinrich); cutlet in aspic with fried potatoes; sauerbrauten with dumplings; puréed peas with boiled beef; pickled boiled beef with horseradish sauce and potatoes, pickled goose with Teltower turnips; boiled beef brisket with horseradish sauce; bouillon potatoes with red beets; sour eggs with bacon sauce and mashed potatoes; and, not to forget another old favorite, Kaiser Jagdwurst with bacon sauce and sour potatoes.

It became customary to eat certain things on certain holidays. On Maundy Thursday it was a sacred custom to eat kale, like eating carp at Christmas and New Year's. Rye was a necessity. The more seeds, the more luck and happiness the New Year would bring. Berlin poppy seed trifles, of Serbian origin, were very popular for the same reason. Berlin jelly doughnuts or pancakes, as the Berliners call them, rank in first place on the list of favorites. The popular cinnamon pretzels used to be enjoyed with coffee or beer, but were replaced by crunchy pretzel sticks and pretzels. Other favorites include the Berlin "Schrippe" and "Knüppel," two types of crunchy rolls, to accompany the morning coffee. The "Schuster-junge," now called "Salzkuchen" or salt cake, are rolls made from ⅔ rye flour, and ⅓ wheat flour. After baking, they are rolled in flour and taste especially good with goose lard and "Harzer" cheese. The name Schusterjunge, which means a shoemaker's apprentice boy, was used in reference to the difference between children of the upper and lower classes. For 1 groschen, one could buy 6 Schusterjungen, but only 4 Schrippen.

Berlin pubs always have a supply of meat patties, rollmops, fried herring, Bismarck herring, and pickled eggs. Meat patties and pickled eggs are eaten with mustard. Nasty tongues claim that these meat patties are just fried Schrippen. Schrippen halves with "Hackepeter" (raw ground pork), diced onions, and a kosher pickle are just as popular as Schrippen with raw ground beef, as a quick, between-meal snack. As always, the usual accompaniment is a "Molle," or beer and a "Korn," or corn schnapps.

The Huguenots, to whom the Berliners owe much, invented the famous "Berliner Weisse mit Schuss." Also popular is the "Weisse mit Strippe," especially favored by men. If you order "mit Strippe" it means that you would like a "Kümmel" or "Allasch" (caraway schnapps) with your beer. In the summer, during outings to the numerous sights in the surrounding area, this drink is consumed in great quantities. It used to be drunk out of special tub-like glasses, which have since been replaced by tall, narrow ones known as "Stupsgläser." Some old-fashioned restaurants, however, are going back to the original "Weissewannen."

The Huguenot Weissbier recipe used barley and wheat flour with a mixture of yeast and lactic acid bacteria, which resulted in this fizzy beer. The Huguenots had previously attempted – unsuccessfully – to grow wine on the Kreuzberg in Berlin. The saying goes that one needed three men to drink this wine – one to drink and two others to hold him up.

Since we are already talking about drinking, we must mention a custom amongst hobby gardeners, namely the Maibowle (May Punch), and the city of Werder's tree blossom festival, which nicely accommodated the Berliner's joy of drinking. The Reichsbahn had to use freight trains to transport the masses that came to enjoy the blossoms and sweet, yet potent, fruit wines.

The dividing of the capital city, as well as the country, have committed these Werder outings to memory only. The same goes for the Stralauer fishermen's parade, which was part of a local celebration dating back to the time when Berlin was still an old fishing village and lasting through the twenties. The fishermen lived on the Stralauer peninsula on Lake Rummelsberg. The parade took place on Bartholomäus Day. The main catch was carp and whitefish. A giant crayfish was always a part of the parade. This noble crustacean, a small lobster, enjoyed considerable admiration and popularity in old Berlin, and lives on in authentic Berlin recipes.

According to an official report of the Berlin central market dated February 1936, 60 nine-centimeter-long crayfish cost RM 1,30. Today one might get one crayfish for that price. Pike perch were sold at 35 to 40 pfennings per pound. At that time, Berlin cuisine was unthinkable without crayfish. There were crayfish tails in dill cream sauce with buttered rice and salad; crayfish were the basis for delicious crayfish soup, and the decorative stuffed crayfish pieces were part of Berlin chicken fricassee as well as Leipziger Allerlei, a vegetable stew made famous in Berlin. Even the crushed shell served as the basis for crab butter. Besides these delicacies caught in local waters, the hearty Matjes herring from the Baltic Sea also deserves mention. Berliners ate Matjes herring with boiled potatoes, green beans, and fresh butter; this was the "people's food" of the prewar years. Today such a "worker's trout" costs DM 1.80. King Wilhelm I of Prussia had the habit of eating his Matjes with boiled potatoes in the court pantry.

Nostalgically remembered by the older generation, the "Bäcker-melone," a type of cake, released wonderful aromas for children's noses. Dusted with powdered sugar, it was the ultimate object of our desires for which we would sacrifice 5 pfennigs of our allowance. Those with lesser means would get a paper bag filled with cake crumbs – almost a ritual for the less fortunate children of Berlin, one never experienced by children of postwar affluence. Pound cake was another favorite. In his novel "Jett'chen Gerbert," the author Herberts writes that you can eat pound cake right up to your own funeral.

In the early twenties, journalists used to gather in the newspaper quarter around Kochstrasse at the world-famous Konditorei Jaedicke, whose owner had been titled "Mundkoch," meaning that he could cook for royalty. Though rarely of the same opinion, the journalists all agreed that it was a matter of honor to eat "Baumkuchen" (tree cake) at Jaedicke's. The centuries-old recipe, made famous in Berlin, was brought to the city by a chimney sweep. He discovered the recipe at a baker's in the Brandenburg Marches, for whom he was working. In Berlin, he had temporary sleeping accommodations at a confectioner's. Upon his departure, as he could not pay for his keep with money, he left the recipe.

In the beginning of the 19th century, the first literary cafés appeared in Berlin and soon became gathering spots for intellectuals. Konditorei Spargnapani became the meeting place for the world's scholars. Stehely's on the Gendarmenmarkt attracted politicians and journalists. In the red room, the national newspaper was founded in the historical year of 1848. The elegant world of aristocrats and courtiers met at Kranzler's on the boulevard "Unter den Linden." In 1870, also on Unter den Linden, the world famous Café Bauer opened with 700 newspapers and magazines at its patrons' disposal. Wine restaurants, truffle, and oyster bars were established, offering refined drinks and tasty snacks. The poet Lessing whiled away the time at Maurer & Brach's in the company of composers Mendelssohn, Nicolai, and Ramler – either involved in serious discussions or bantering. The establishments Lutter and Wegener became world famous through the patronage of E. T. A. Hoffmann and his friend Ludwig Devrient.

Then came the beer palaces, the authentic Berlin distilleries, pubs, and beer saloons. This was where the carriage drivers in their wide coats, porters, and soot-covered factory workers stood at bar counters guzzling their beers and corn schnapps.

In the evening hours, along the banks of the Spree River, one could see the brightly illuminated castle and the many windows of the court kitchen, behind which the various royal cooks hustled and bustled about. Major foreign embassies were located at Pariser Platz, in front of the Brandenburg Gate. They were considered temples of fine cuisine. The Weinstuben Habel, on Unter den Linden, was founded by Frederick the Great's cellarer. It was frequented by ministers and generals. The legendary establishment Adlon, on Pariser Platz, was built by the businessman Conrad Uhl. It was the ne plus ultra at the time and served celebrities from all over the world. Those who experienced the ambiance and graciousness of these establishments could consider themselves extremely fortunate. The most illustrious chefs were in service here.

The grand Hotel Bristol was located near the Adlon. Across from the Café Bauer was the restaurant "Unter den Linden." Here the boiled beef brisket was served from a cart with horseradish sauce and bouillon potatoes. The great stage actor Heinrich George was a regular there.

The magnificent wine restaurant Kaiser-Keller was on Friedrichstrasse; it is hard to imagine that something like that ever existed.

Steps away, on the corner of Friedrichstrasse and Leipziger Strasse, the wine restaurant Kempinski employed 250 cooks. The salary of a chef would have made many a privy councillor green with envy. Three tons of lobster, 30,000 crayfish, 200 kilograms of caviar, and 20,000 oysters were used daily. Per day, 18,000 rolls, baked in the restaurant's own bakery, were consumed. They broke 40,000 plates annually. The Kempinski served rabbit and pheasant the day after the opening of the hunt in Bohemia.

Fresh oysters and lobsters were delivered twice a day. At the time, Berlin's cuisine was at a peak never to be achieved again. In 1930,

10 blue point oysters cost RM 2.00; 10 Imperiales RM 3.20; an oyster cocktail RM 0.75; ½ cold lobster with tartar sauce (Sauce Remoulade) RM 2.50; young pheasant with goose liver purée RM 2.00; a Châteaubriand for two RM 4.00; 3 thrushes with sauerkraut and croutons RM 2.35.

At the turn of the century, the Zentralhotel was built by the railroad station on Friedrichstrasse. At the time it was the largest and most beautiful hotel in Berlin. Next to it was the Russischer Hof, with its world-famous "Wintergarten," and across from it the unforgettable "Franziskaner" restaurant that served international and Berlin cuisine. The cooks busily prepared 3000 to 4000 meals daily. The small menu, served on a silver plate, came to RM 1.35; the larger menu was RM 2.10. Even the soup was served in a silver bowl. Those were the days.

The wine restaurant Borchardt was south of Friedrichstrasse. The most extraordinary of delicacies could be found here. Privy Councillor von Holstein was a regular at this house of gourmet cuisine. Not far away, on Lutherstrasse, was the wine restaurant Horcher, a Luculan temple frequented by top government officials. Also worth noting are the renowned establishments "Prinz Wilhelm," "Taubenkasino," "Töpfer," and "Prinz Friedrich Karl." The "Imperator," known as the "house of 1000 easy chairs," it also memorable. Kurt Widmann, Berlin's Tommy Dorsey, made a name for himself here.

Nearby, on Maurerstrasse, was the "Clou," a house of festivities. Farther south was the lovely "Moka-Efti" with its famous five-o'clock tea. Bernhard Etté and Erhard Bauschke performed here; their act was transmitted by the Königswusterhausen radio station. The exquisite "Faun" was located across from the Moka-Efti. "Die Traube," another wine restaurant, was on Leipziger Strasse, not far from the huge department store Wertheim. For originality, visitors to Berlin were always taken to the "Haus Vaterland" on Potsdamer Platz. This establishment housed several eateries including the "Berliner Budicke," "Teltower Rübchen," "Bayrischer Löwenbräu," "Wien-Grinzing," "Chinesische Teestube," "Italienische Piazetta," "Wildwest Bar," "Türkisches Cafe," "Rheinterrasse," and "Palmensaal." Forty-five cooks were employed here for the culinary delight of the patrons. Other lager beer halls included the "Pschorr am Potsdamer Platz," the "Spatenbräu," the "Heidelberger," the "Weihenstephan," and the "Klaussner." The distinguished hotel "Fürstenhof" stood across from the Pschorr. At the entrance of the Berlin zoo was the first-class hotel "Esplanade," famous for its magnificent ballrooms such as the Mirror Room. The Esplanade's cuisine was considered among the most popular and famous in Berlin.

On the opposite side of town, at the Anhalter railroad station, stood a colossal structure, the "super hotel Excelsior," owned by Privy Councillor Elschner. It was the largest hotel on the continent with 600 rooms, 700 beds, 250 baths, and 700 employees of which 85 were cooks. It had a seating capacity of 5000 and was connected directly to the Anhalter train station by elevators and tunnels. This is quite impressive, even by today's spaceage standards. In the Excelsior's "Thomas Keller" restaurant, in 1936, one paid RM 1.25 for roast goose with red cabbage and dumplings. A double corn schnapps was at RM 0.30. The well-known first-class hotel "Kaiserhof" on the Wilhelmsplatz luxuriously harbored guests from all around the world. Its banquet halls were always in demand. The "Eden-Hotel" on Budapester Strasse was also an international, first-rate establishment. It was famous for its cuisine, which ranked among the best in Berlin, producing first-class chefs. The Eden had an attractive rooftop restaurant, whose glass roof could be opened automatically. The international dance bands that performed there attracted the patronage of the rich and the beautiful. The Berlin zoo grounds housed the restaurant "Kroll," a popular meeting place for all Berliners. Another Kempinski restaurant on the Kurfürstendamm had its last heyday during the 1936 Olympics. Then all the glitter was snuffed out by the eternal night of war. Old menus document the high standard of this establishment.

Our stroll through old Berlin should not end without mentioning one of its largest gastronomic enterprises, MITROPA, the largest hotel and restaurant on wheels. Its 450 chefs, 200 in Berlin area alone, were shining examples of duty and efficiency.

These chefs needed sure footing; the "flying zeppelins on wheels," the trains "Fliegender Breslauer" and "Fliegender Beuthener" traveled at a top speed of 200 km/h, which means that it took 1¾ hours to travel from Berlin to Breslau. One hundred additional trips with salon cars for official government business such as state visits, etc. were made annually.

This Berlin no longer exists. All of the establishments mentioned here went under in the inferno of the last war. The cream of almost an entire generation of chefs, who had bestowed many hours of enjoyment upon so many people, disappeared, many of them practicing their profession as army cooks on the battlefields of Europe.

Prussia was dissolved by order of the Allied Control Council. All that remains is the Prussian Cultural Foundation which is instrumental in maintaining the cultural heritage, including culinary traditions and customs.

Cookbooks are cultural documents that sometimes reflect their times better and more eloquently than history books. Although the latter may never be completely without bias, cookbooks certainly are.

And now, dear reader, we have completed our stroll. I have attempted to put together the necessary ingredients for preparing dishes for four persons according to the old recipes as was customary in old Berlin. I herewith lay down a wreath in memory of Berlin, the temple of culinary art. Many a Berliner, either here or far away, will, while reading this book, nostalgically concede that he still has "einen Koffer in Berlin," or a suitcase in Berlin.

In Berlin they work hard, but they play hard, too. And should someone "on the outside" suddenly feel homesick for the Kurfürstendamm, then the book has hit its mark!

Good luck with the recipes, and guten Appetit!

27

fig. 2

Ambrosia

This was a favorite drink of the young Heinrich Heine, who was, as we know, quite a "Schmecklecker" or gourmet.

In his letters he describes his expeditions through old Berlin and mentions this delicious "drink of the Gods."

He also notes that the meringues at Jagor's were even sweeter than this – as though Aphrodite had emerged from their sweet foam. They were filled with a variety of flavored whipped creams including vanilla, "Waldmeister," strawberry, and orange.

He sat in the crowded café with his friends Josty and Devrient, drinking the sweet ambrosia.

> *½ liter sweet cream, 50 grams vanilla sugar, ¼ liter fresh, strained strawberries, 1 small glass good-quality kirsch, 1 glass Madeira, 150 grams fresh, diced pineapple.*

Rub the fresh strawberries through a sieve and stir well with the sugar.

Beat the cream, but do not let it get too stiff.

Now mix the lightly whipped cream with the strawberries, pour into a container and place in the freezer to chill. It should not harden. Then stir again and mix in the liqueur.

Shortly before serving, mix in the diced pineapple and serve in flat, preferably stemmed glasses. Place dessert spoons alongside.

Jenny Lind Punch

This was a fashionable drink in Berlin around the turn of the 19th century. It was named after Jenny Lind, "the Swedish nightingale." In "Stechlin," Fontane describes this punch, which he drank during a stopover at an old inn in Berlin-Treptow.

This brings back memories. What Berliner does not remember Sunday family outings of this inn, the "Altes Eierhäuschen," with its wonderful playground and miniature train.

2 oranges, 200 grams sugar cubes, 2 bottles Rhein wine, ¼ vanilla bean, ¼ liter Madeira.

Rub the sugar cubes over the rind of one (unsprayed) orange. Then squeeze both oranges and boil the juice with the sugar. Add both bottles of wine, boil again, and remove from heat. Slit the vanilla bean and add to the liquid. Cool. Then strain, add Madeira. Cool again before serving.

Kaiser Tea

This old tea recipe was a favorite of Wilhelm, the last German emperor, and his wife Auguste-Viktoria.

4 egg yolks, 1 full liqueur glass maraschino, 4–5 table-spoons sugar, orange pekoe tea.

The original recipe called for "caravan tea" that has not lost its flavor to the ocean air. It is exceptionally tasty.

In a heated teapot, add 4 teaspoons of tea and cover with 4 glasses boiling water. Cover and steep for 2 to 3 minutes. Stir well. Mix the egg yolks with the maraschino in a porcelain teapot. Then add the tea poured through a tea sieve, and stir again.

Serve in heated tea glasses or cups and add granulated sugar, sugar cubes, or rock sugar to taste.

Rose Wine

In the past, roses were considered a delicate taste enhancer. Perhaps they can be that again?

It is well worth the effort to dig up an old recipe from Sanssouci's court kitchen; it is said that they had the most beautiful roses. Imagine "old Fritz," sitting in candlelight or perhaps amidst a circle of friends, smoking and drinking sparkling rose wine from lovely glasses.

The original recipe, from near Fulda, dates from the year 400 and so found its way into our culture.

(By the way, were you aware that Frederick was also a coffee gourmet? Instead of water, he sometimes boiled champagne for his coffee. Try it!)

Use petals from four large roses. Remove the white parts and wrap petals in a clean white cloth. Place in a bowl and pour in contents of one bottle of white wine. Cover and let stand for seven days. Remove, add another bottle of white wine, one or two spoonfuls sugar water or, even better, honey. Mix well.

Ask Ingrid, she knows how to make it

Waldmeister (Woodruff) Punch

In a bowl with two bottles of Mosel or Rhein wine, place a fresh bouquet of woodruff, which gives the punch its inimitable aroma and flavor. Woodruff grows wild in forests and gardens; it should be cut before it blossoms. It contains coumarin, the aroma of which is released after soaking in the wine for half an hour.

After removing the bouquet, add crystal sugar dissolved in boiling water, but be careful not to oversweeten.

Then add two small glasses of cognac and half a bottle of sparkling wine. Enhance with a few orange slices.

Cover, cool, and serve.

The German name for punch (Bowle) stems from "Bolle," a round container in which the drink is prepared.

Flower punches – such as violet, rose, and acacia – were also common. Although largely unknown today, they are prepared in the same way.

Celery punch was also popular. Celery root was soaked in wine and removed before serving. Another forgotten drink is the once popular cucumber punch, prepared with red wine.

Palace Punch

Recipe from the chef of the royal kitchen at the city palace at the Lustgarten.

For 4 persons:

1 bottle white wine (Rhein, Mosel, Saar, or Ruwer), ⅛ liter high-proof rum, ¼ liter water, 200 grams granulated sugar, 75-gram sugar cone, 1 small piece of cinnamon.

Dissolve the granulated sugar in the boiling water. Add the white wine. Place the sugar cone over the top of the punch bowl, saturate with rum, light with a match, and let drip into punch. Add the piece of cinnamon. Then gradually add rum.

It is customary to drink the punch hot in winter and chilled in the summer.

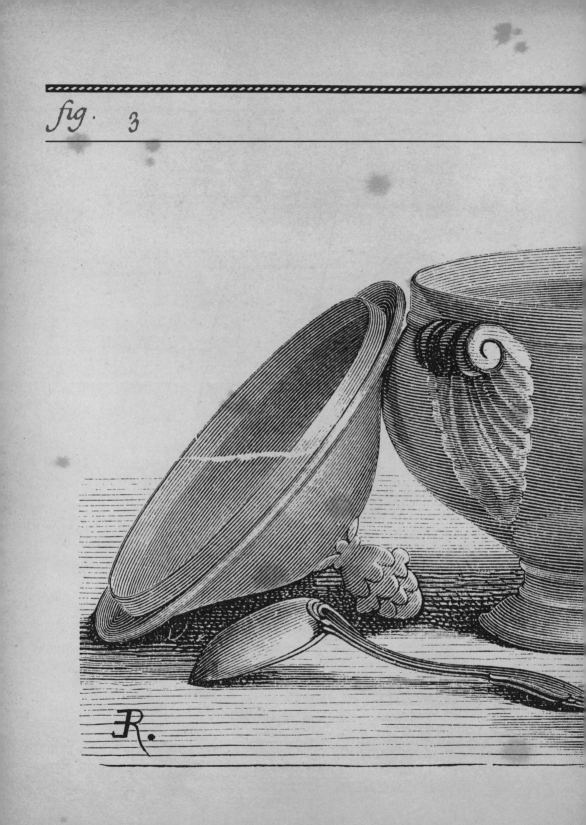

fig. 3

C. LAPLANTE

Cold Beer Soup

100 grams currants, 100 grams sugar, 75 grams zwieback crumbs, 75 grams black bread crumbs, 1 liter weiss beer, ½ lemon (cut in slices), a dash of cinnamon.

Soak currants for a few hours. Add the beer and remaining ingredients.

Refrigerate for a few hours, then serve in glasses or bowls.

Raisins may be used instead of currants.

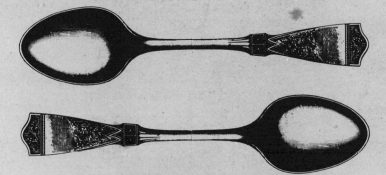

Barley Soup with Dried Prunes
(a traditional lunch or dinner dish)

250 grams barley, 250 grams prunes, 1 tablespoon sugar or syrup, 50 grams butter, 300 grams smoked meat or leftover roast, some cinnamon, some salt.

In a covered pot, boil the barley in salted water with butter flakes. Stir frequently, occasionally adding water. Simmer slowly until tender.

Meanwhile, cover the prunes with water and cook with the sugar until soft. Mix with the soft barley and season to taste.

Serve in deep dishes, sprinkle with cinnamon sugar, and top with brown butter.

Serve cold smoked meat or roast as a side dish.

The barley soup should be just thick enough to eat with a fork.

Berlin Potato Soup

350 grams peeled potatoes, 80 grams soup greens: leek, celery, carrots, 1 onion, 1 liter light beef broth, 50 grams diced lean bacon, ⅛ liter sweet or sour cream, approx. 30 grams flour, 1 small bay leaf, 4 pimientos, ½ teaspoon caraway seeds, 2 crushed juniper berries, some marjoram, a dash of mace, salt, pepper, 30 grams butter, 2 slices white bread (diced), chopped parsley, chervil leaves.

Sauté the bacon. Add the finely chopped soup greens, diced onion, and potatoes cut in small pieces. Stir, and add beef broth. Add spices, cover, and simmer for approx. half an hour.

Strain and bring to a boil. Mix cream with flour. Bind soup with this mixture. Season to taste with salt and freshly ground pepper.

Add butter to saucepan; when foamy, add diced white bread and brown lightly until crisp. Shortly before serving, sprinkle over soup and garnish with chopped parsley and chervil.

To round it off, you may wish to add frankfurters, wieners, or Bockwurst. It is also common in Berlin to use strips of boiled beef.

Crayfish Soup

20 crayfish, 150 grams finely chopped soup greens: celery, carrots, leek, 1 chopped onion, some caraway seeds, 50 grams flour, 50 grams butter, ⅛ liter cream, some sweet paprika, 100 grams fish (preferably pike), 1 egg, 1 liter beef bouillon, 2 tablespoons boiled green peas, approx. 8 boiled asparagus tips, salt, pepper, cayenne pepper, mace, 1 slice of white bread, vinegar, sugar, lemon juice, a dash of cognac, some chopped dillweed.

Clean crayfish well. Bring beef bouillon to a boil and add the live crayfish one by one. After 5 minutes, remove with a slotted spoon and break open. Remove meat from claws and tails. Remove stomach and intestinal vein.

In a blender, chop the shells together with the soup greens, the onion, caraway seeds, and paprika. Sauté this mixture in foaming butter, dust with flour, and add the stock. Simmer for approx. 20 minutes, strain and set aside.

Grind the fish meat and mix with egg, salt, pepper, mace, soaked white bread, and cream to make a fish farce. Make small dumplings with a teaspoon and drop in boiling salted water with a bit of vinegar added. Simmer.

Pour the fish stock into the crayfish stock and bind with cream. Season with salt, a pinch of cayenne pepper, a pinch of sugar, lemon juice, and a dash of cognac.

Serve in soup bowls with the fish dumplings, crayfish meat, green peas, and asparagus tips. Top with fresh dillweed.

It is delightful.

Peas with Pork

½ pickled pig's head, 400 grams unpeeled yellow peas, 100 grams peeled potatoes, 80 grams soup greens, 40 grams flour, 75 grams lean bacon, some salt, pepper, sugar, majoran, bay leaf, 1 pimiento, 2 onions.

Cover pig's head with water, add a pinch of sugar, one whole onion, the bay leaf, and pimiento. Cook the head until tender, but not so that it falls apart. Debone and set aside.

Strain the stock and use to cook washed peas and the finely chopped soup greens. If too salty, dilute with water.

Stir the peas occasionally until tender. Shortly before they are ready, add the diced potatoes.

Lightly sauté the diced lean bacon in a pan with the chopped onion. Rub in some marjoram, add the flour, stir well and add to the soup to bind. Season to taste with salt and pepper.

Now add pieces of pig's ears and snout and serve with crunchy rolls. You may also add sausage such as Bockwurst.

Warm Beer Soup

This is really a very traditional meal. Even Frederick the Great, or "Alter Fritz" (old Fritz) as he was affectionately called, was raised on beer soup.

At the time, coffee was forbidden as it was considered a vice. A 1780 ordinance praised the virtues of brandy and beer. It called for the destruction of any pots, cups, dishes, coffee mills, burners, and anything else to do with coffee, so that no one should be reminded of it. Violators risked imprisonment.

Here, rescued from obscurity, is the Frederickan beer soup recipe:

> *¾ liter not-too-bitter beer and equal amount of water, approx. 45 grams finely sifted flour (not potato flour), 3 whole eggs, sugar to taste, a dash of cinnamon, 1 lemon wedge, 1½ cups dried white bread croutons or the same amount of zwieback, 50 grams butter.*

Mix all ingredients except white bread and butter in a pot. Stir constantly over high heat with a whisk. Just before the boiling point, pour into a soup terrine. Then lightly brown the croutons in butter and add to the soup.

It used to be common to soak currants in beer, sauté leftover black bread in butter, add some fine sugar and a dash of cinnamon and knead these ingredients into a dough. This dough was squeezed through a funnel into a soup terrine and then covered with the beer soup.

39

Notes and more recipes

Notes and more recipes

fig. 4

C. LAPLANTE

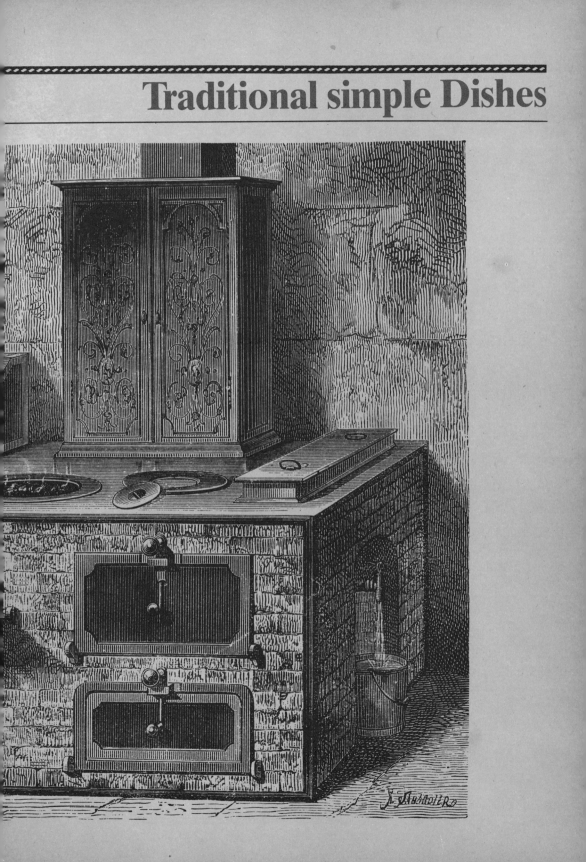

Mama's Knödel Recipe.

Yeast Dumplings with Cooked Fruit

As a variation of the dish "Schlesisches Himmelreich," it became customary in Berlin to cook yeast dumplings with dried fruit because some people did not care for the combination of sweet dried fruit with smoked bacon.

Whenever there was cooked fruit and yeast dumplings, it required little effort on our mother's part to get us to the table.

350 grams dried fruit, some sugar, a piece of cinnamon stick, some grated gingerbread.
For the dumplings:
375 grams sifted flour, ¼ liter milk, 2 whole eggs, a pinch of salt, nutmeg, 30 grams fresh yeast, 35 grams soft butter.
50 grams butter and some dried white bread crumbs to sprinkle over the dumplings.

Pour the flour in a bowl and make a well in the center, in which to mix the milk and yeast. Then arrange the remaining ingredients around the rim of the bowl along with the beaten eggs. After the starter has risen, work everything into a dough and roll out into a long loaf. Slice off equal-sized pieces and form these into dumplings. Let rise in a warm place. Meanwhile, bring a pot of water to a boil. When the dumplings are ready, simmer in the boiling water to for approx. 5 minutes on either side. Brown the bread crumbs in hot butter and pour over the dumplings. Serve with a portion of hot, cooked fruit prepared according to the recipe for "Schlesisches Himmelreich" (page 45).

The above recipe was also popular in Niederlausitz from where it made its way to Berlin.

Boiled Potatoes with Farmers' Cheese and Linseed Oil

Although most people think this recipe originated in Berlin, it actually stems from Silesia, just as every other Berliner in the old days was actually from Silesia. Here again we have cultural and historical proof that Berlin cuisine is in fact a conglomeration of that of its environs. Berlin, the former German capital, has always been made up of a mixture of Germans from all over the country. This variety is reflected in its cuisine.

1 kilogram small or medium-sized potatoes, 1 teaspoon salt, 1 teaspoon caraway seeds, 500 grams low-fat farmers' cheese, 2 tablespoons milk, 2 medium-sized onions, some pepper, 2–3 tablespoons linseed oil, 80 grams fresh butter, 1 small bunch curly parsley.

Wash the potatoes well and place in boiling water with salt and caraway seeds. Cover and simmer for 20–25 minutes. While the potatoes are cooking, mix the farmers' cheese with milk and season to taste with salt and pepper.

Make a well in the cheese and fill with the finely chopped onions. Pour over the linseed oil, top with freshly ground pepper and garnish with the sprigs of curly parsley. Cut the butter into portions and place around the edge. Peel the potatoes and serve lightly salted, together with the farmers' cheese.

Schlesisches Himmelreich

As the name implies, this dish comes from Silesia, the land of Rübezahl, the spirit of the Sudeten Mountains. This was "Old Fritz's" favorite province. By the turn of the century, every third Berliner came from Silesia – a "Rucksackberliner" (carpetbagger) in Berlin vernacular. No wonder this dish originated in Berlin – not in Silesia.

600 grams lean smoked bacon or meat, 250 grams mixed dried fruit, leftover boiled potatoes, 40 grams butter, some fine dried white bread crumbs, sugar, cinnamon, some grated gingerbread, 1 egg, salt, nutmeg, some flour.

Soak the dried fruit in water overnight. The next day, using the same water, add some sugar and a small piece of cinnamon stick and cook until soft. Then add the grated gingerbread to thicken.

At the same time, place the smoked meat or lean bacon in cold water and cook until done.

45

Put the cold, peeled potatoes through a ricer and make a dumpling dough with egg, salt, a bit of nutmeg, and flour. Add as much flour as the mixture can absorb. Roll into round dumplings, which are cooked in gently boiling salted water for 15 minutes.

Serve the dumplings with a portion of hot cooked fruit, and 2 small slices of smoked meat. Make a light Polonaise sauce using the dry bread crumbs and butter. Pour a bit over each dumpling.

Grandma's Berlin Kosher Pickles

Take 5 liters well water and dissolve in it, the day before, 225 grams salt. Wash 5 pounds pickling cucumbers and soak overnight in well water.

> *10 grams basil, 40 grams cherry tree leaves, 40 grams grape leaves, 4 grams peppercorns, 70 grams dried dillweed.*

Place alternate layers of spices and pickles in the brine which should cover the pickles. Push down with a wooden top so that the pickles stay under the brine.

Remove the scum with a ladle. In 2 weeks you will have delicious pickles.

Notes and more recipes

fig. 5

Vegetables

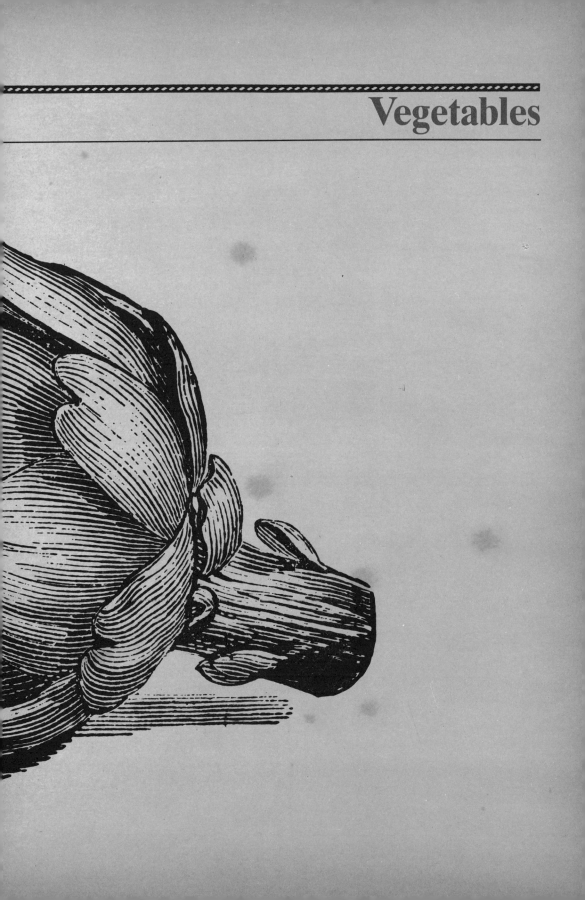

Bouillon Potatoes

*1 kilogram peeled potatoes, 1 liter good beef bouil-
lon, 100 grams mixture of carrots, celery root, leek,
1 teaspoon chopped caraway seeds, salt, pepper, nutmeg, parsley.*

This typical spicy potato side-dish is usually served with boiled
beef – or pickled beef brisket with horseradish sauce and red
beets. This is why you should use good beef broth.

The preparation is relatively easy.

Cut the peeled potatoes in 3×3 cm cubes. Drop in boiling water
for a few minutes and then add to the gently boiling beef broth.
Cook for approx. 10 minutes at low heat with the finely chopped
vegetables and caraway seeds. Immediately remove from heat and
season with salt, pepper, and nutmeg.

Serve topped with chopped parsley.

Berlin Potato Pancakes

This is yet another popular, simple dish which every Berliner is
happy to eat as long as it does not mean grating the potatoes. The
"Kartoffelpuffer" are today still sold on the street at snack stands.

*1 kilogram peeled, large potatoes, 2–3 eggs and salt,
120 grams pork lard for frying, 1–2 tablespoons
flour.*

Soak the peeled potatoes in water, then grate into a bowl. Pour in
a small amount of the potato water and add salt. Stir in flour and
2 to 3 eggs. Heat the lard in a skillet. Place spoonfuls of the potato
mixture in the skillet and form into wide patties. Gently brown on
both sides and serve.

Season to taste with sugar or salt and serve with apple sauce, cranberries, or pumpkin compote. In Berlin it is customary to drink
hot coffee with potato pancakes.

If you prefer heartier potato pancakes, sauté diced lean bacon before adding the pancakes to the pan. Then place a slice of raw onion on the pancake. The onion will fry with the pancake when it is turned over.

Puréed Peas

500 grams peeled yellow peas, 1 piece of ham or bacon rind, 1 large peeled potato, salt, pepper, 75 grams lean bacon, 1 large onion.

Soak the peas overnight. Cook, well covered with water, together with the bacon or ham rind added, for approx. 1 hour until tender.

Stir frequently with a wooden spoon to prevent burning.

Shortly before the peas are done, add the potato in small pieces and cook with the peas until tender. Then put everything through a ricer, stir well, and season to taste with salt and pepper.

The puréed peas should have the consistency of mashed potatoes.

Cut the bacon in cubes and sauté. Add the diced onion, sauté until transparent, then pour a spoonful over each portion of purée.

This hearty side dish is usually served with pigs' knuckles and pickled pork.

It is also customary to serve with one or two potato halves.

Steamed Cucumbers

This mild, quickly prepared dish calls for large cucumbers. Preparation time is approx. 15 minutes.

1 kilogram cucumbers, ¼ liter milk, 60 grams butter, 50 grams flour, 1 tablespoon sugar, 1 tablespoon vinegar, salt, pepper.

Pare and seed the cucumbers. Cut lengthwise into finger-thick slices.

Melt the butter in a pan. Add sugar, dust with flour, then add in cucumber slices. Let draw, stirring constantly, then add milk.

Cover and steam for approx. 15 minutes. Season with salt, pepper, vinegar, and more sugar, if necessary.

Leipziger Allerlei

This vegetable dish is best in the spring and during asparagus season.

200 grams diced kohlrabi, 200 grams cleaned young carrots, 200 grams green peas, 200 grams peeled asparagus, ¼ liter beef broth, 1 medium-sized cauliflower, 1 cup milk, salt, sugar, 200 grams morels, butter, 12 crayfish, some root vegetables, caraway seeds, 1 bay leaf.
For the crayfish filling:
50 grams butter, 2 egg yolks, 2 egg whites, 50 grams breadcrumbs, salt, pepper, nutmeg.
For the sauce:
60 grams butter, 50 grams flour, 2 egg yolks, some cream.

Place the kohlrabi, carrots, and green peas separately in light beef broth with a dash of salt and sugar and steam until tender. Cut the asparagus into finger-long pieces and also steam in the bouillon. Cut the cauliflower into florets and cook in milk and water until tender. Cook the morels in salted water first, then steam until tender in a small saucepan with butter.

Meanwhile, place the root vegetables, bayleaf, and caraway seeds in vigorously boiling salted water. Then add the crayfish and boil for 15 minutes.

Remove meat from the claws and tail and eviscerate. Set aside the cavity for the filling. Heat the remaining crushed shells with the butter over moderate heat to make crayfish butter. Strain after 25 minutes.

Mix the stirred butter with the egg yolks, the beaten egg whites, and breadcrumbs. Season with salt, pepper, and nutmeg. Replace in the shell and make small dumplings with the excess. Simmer both in the stock until tender.

Now make a sauce with the various vegetable broths and the cauliflower milk. Make a light roux with the butter and the flour. Add broth for the desired thickness, stirring constantly with a whisk. Stir in the egg yolks and some sweet cream as the final touch. Season with salt, pepper, nutmeg, and a dash of sugar. Arrange the warm vegetables on a hot platter with the cauliflower in the center, surrounded alternately by the other vegetables. Arrange the crayfish meat, stuffed shells, and dumplings alternately on top of the vegetables.

Brush the vegetables with the crayfish butter.

As the preparation of this noble dish is rather time consuming and costly, it is certainly still a luxury.

Asparagus Spears

2 kilograms white asparagus spears, 200 grams fresh butter, 1 lemon wedge, parsley.

Peel the asparagus from the head down. Cut off the lower part of the stalk and place in boiling water with an unsprayed lemon wedge. Cover and simmer for approx. 25 minutes until tender, then add salt to taste. Drain well, brush with butter, and garnish around the tips with chopped parsley.

Serve with fresh or melted butter, buttered parsley potatoes, or thin slices of ham.

Asparagus Spears in Dill Cream Sauce

2 kilograms asparagus spears, 1 small lemon wedge, 100 grams sweet cream butter, 60 grams flour, 1 cup sweet cream, 2 bunches fresh dill, 2 egg yolks, salt, pepper, sugar, a dash of nutmeg.

Peel the asparagus as usual and place in boiling water with a flake of butter and a lemon wedge. Cover and cook until tender for about 25 minutes.

Prepare a light roux with the flour and sweet cream butter. Stirring constantly, add as much asparagus liquid as necessary. Cook and stir the sauce slowly for about 10 minutes. Fold in the egg yolks mixed with cream, remove from heat, and season to taste with salt, a bit of pepper, nutmeg, and some sugar. Before serving, mix in the chopped dill. Pour this delicious sauce over the drained asparagus. Serve with extra sauce and parsley potatoes.

Teltower Turnips

This is a genuine Brandenburg vegetable. It is season in October/November.

Goethe liked these turnips so much that he had his friends in Berlin send them to him every year at his residence in Weimar.

Below is an old Berlin recipe:

900 grams Teltower turnips, 70 grams butter, 1 heaping tablespoon sugar, 40 grams flour, 1/4 liter beef broth, salt, pepper.

Melt the butter over low heat in a large pan. Add the sugar and let caramelize until it turns light brown. Dust with flour and stir with a wooden spatula until the mixture takes on a bit of color. Now add the peeled, washed, whole turnips, stirring constantly, until they too acquire a bit of color. Add the boiling beef broth with a bit of salt and stir well. Cover and simmer slowly for approx. 1½ hours. Season to taste when done.

Serve with any freshly slaughtered meat or sausages, tongue, duck, roasted goose, or smoked meat.

Notes and more recipes

fig. 6

Old Fashioned Bacon and Egg Pancakes with Salad

This dish is especially popular in the spring.

240 grams flour, ½ liter weiss beer, 6 eggs, salt,
a dash of nutmeg, 1 pinch of baking powder.
For frying: 120 grams fatty bacon cubes.

Pour the flour into the beer and stir with a whisk until smooth. Then stir in eggs, spices, and baking powder.

Per pancake, fry 30 grams of bacon in a skillet until crunchy. Pour in pancake batter with a ladle. Brown on both sides.

The less experienced may use a spatula to flip the pancakes.

Serve the pancakes immediately accompanied with lettuce tossed in vinegar, oil, salt, pepper, sugar, finely chopped onions, freshly chopped parsley, and fresh dill.

Hoppel-Poppel

This is a typical Berlin expression. The dish probably stems from the imagination of a professional cook. Since the turn of the century, the Berlin Association of Cooks has had a bowling club named Hoppel-Poppel.

400 grams pork and veal schnitzel leftovers, 1 onion,
1 teaspoon caraway seeds, salt, pepper, chopped
parsley, 600 grams cold, peeled boiled potatoes,
12 eggs, 1 kosher pickle, 125 grams butter.

Slice the potatoes into 2 centimeters thick cubes and fry in butter until golden brown.

In a separate, very hot pan, fry the schnitzel meat in strips with some butter. Season with salt and pepper. As soon as the meat is fried, add the diced onion and mix. Prepare 4 meat portions, then take another pan, melt 25 grams butter, add one portion of meat and mix.

Pour 3 beaten eggs over the meat. Mix again. Form into an omelette, top with parsley, and serve with few slices of kosher pickles on the side. Prepare all meat portions in the same manner. You may also wish to pour over some leftover gravy.

Boiled Eggs with Mustard Sauce

8 eggs, 50 grams butter, 50 grams flour, ¼ liter beef broth, ⅛ liter milk, approx. 50 grams mustard, salt, pepper, sugar, 1 bay leaf, 4 pimientos.

Boil the beef broth with the spices. Heat the milk. Make a roux with the butter and flour. Add the beef broth and stir until smooth. Then stir in the milk and mustard. Season with salt, pepper, a dash of sugar, add vinegar, if necessary.

Pour the sauce in a bowl with the peeled 5-minute-eggs and serve with mashed potatoes and lettuce.

Sour Eggs with Bacon Sauce

8 eggs, 70 grams lean bacon, 50 grams flour, 1 onion, ⅜ liter beef broth, 3 tablespoons sour cream, salt, pepper, sugar, vinegar, 1 bunch parsley.

Dice the bacon and sauté in a saucepan. Add the diced onion and sauté until transparent. Add the flour to make a roux. Pour in the beef broth and stir. Season with a dash of vinegar, salt, pepper, and sugar, then add the cream. Bring water with a dash of vinegar and salt to a boil and crack in the eggs one by one. Simmer for 9 minutes, drain, and serve in a bowl with the bacon sauce accompanied by mashed potatoes and sprinkled with parsley.

Notes and more recipes

Notes and more recipes

fig · 7

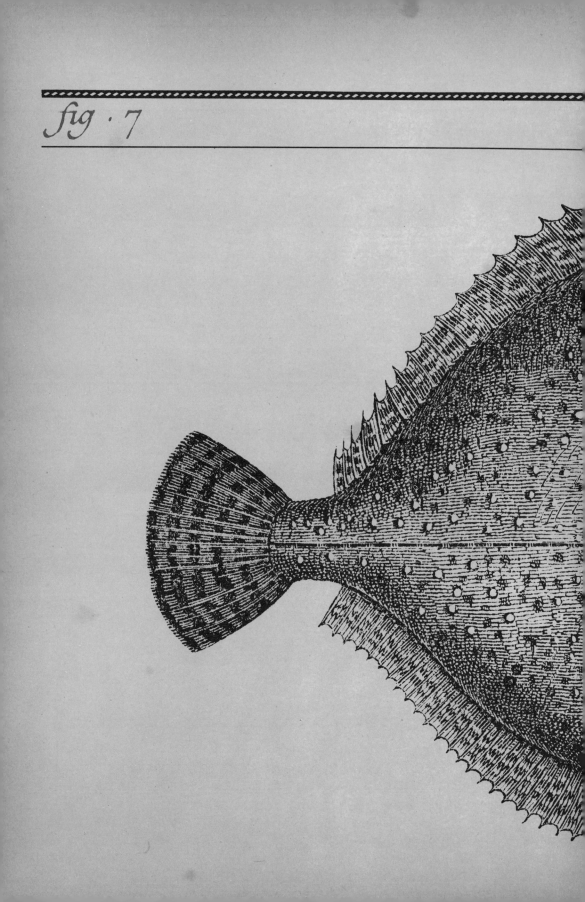

Fish Dishes

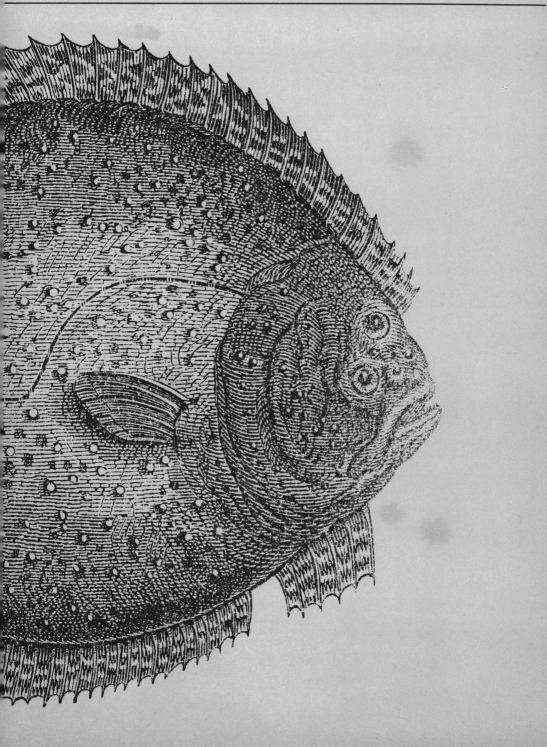

Fried Grass Pike

The grass pike is a small pike weighing approx. 300 grams. In the prewar years, every household in Berlin kept a steady supply of this fish. Today it is almost extinct.

Naturally, you will need four fish for four people. Scale, remove entrails, and clean. Do not chop off the head. Slash the skin on either side three or four times. Season with salt, pepper, lemon juice, and Worcester sauce. Roll in flour and fry in a skillet with hot butter, turning frequently, until golden brown.

Serve on a long platter. Cover with thin slices of peeled lemon, top with chopped parsley, and drizzle with brown butter.

Accompany with buttered potatoes, or warm bacon and potato salad and green salad with fresh dill.

Pike in Spreewälder Sauce

Every Berliner has been to the Spree Forest at least once. The cuisine from this area quickly found acceptance in the old German capital. Sour cucumbers, pickled Spree Forest-style, are still found today in the pubs of Berlin.

1 kilogram cleaned and scaled pike, 2 tablespoons vinegar, 1 bay leaf, 5 pimientos, salt, pepper, 1 lemon, 1 parsley root, 75 grams carrots, 75 grams celery root, 50 grams leek, 1 large onion, 1 bunch chopped parsley, 75 grams butter, 50 grams flour, ⅛ liter sweet cream, 2 egg yolks.

Bring to a boil approx. 1 liter water with vinegar, bay leaf, pimiento, parsley, and sufficient salt. Add the cleaned and filleted fish and simmer for approx. 15 minutes until tender.

Meanwhile, cut the carrots, celery, leek, and onion into matchsticksize slices and sauté briefly in 25 grams butter. Add water or fish stock, cover, and simmer slowly. Prepare a roux with rest of butter and the flour, adding strained pike stock as necessary, stirring constantly to keep smooth. After 10 minutes, stir in the vegetable strips and bind with the beaten egg yolks mixed with cream.

Season to taste with salt, pepper, and lemon juice.

Pour the sauce over the fish and top with parsley. Serve with boiled or dill potatoes and green salads.

Good for company.

Fried Pike with Potato Salad

This dish brings back memories of the now almost extinct "Volksfest" in the tiny fishing village Stralau, near Treptow. It was also native to Niederlausitz. The pike is a predator still found in the waters in and around Berlin. This fish can grow to a length of two meters and weigh up to 35 kilograms.

> *80 grams cleaned pike fillet, salt, pepper, 1 lemon, 2 eggs, some flour, dry bread crumbs, 100 grams butter for frying.*

Cut 4 equal-sized pike fillets. Rinse briefly and season with salt, pepper, and lemon juice. Let draw for approx. 10 minutes, then roll in flour. Dip the fillets in the beaten eggs, then coat with bread crumbs. Fry in hot butter until golden brown on both sides.

Serve with lemon wedges and buttered or dill potatoes. (Toss the hot potatoes in melted butter with freshly chopped dill.) Also good with lettuce and cucumber salad or brown or melted butter, as pike is a very lean fish. With a fat content of 0.3%, 100 grams pike have only 45 calories.

In the country it is also customary to bake the pike with plenty of butter, salt and pepper, with sour cream added shortly before it is done.

Pike Dumplings

This recipe is from the recipe collection of the noble kitchen of the Counts of Waldersee whose family tree dates directly back to the famous Dessauer, or "old Dessauer", as he was called. I had the privilege to serve as cook in the house of the young countess Gabriele Waldersee. One member of this truly noble house was an aide-de-camp under King Wilhelm, while another was chamberlain at the court of Emperor Wilhelm II. Countess Gabriele's great uncle was the legendary field marshall Count Waldersee, commander-in-chief of the German allied troups which stifled the Boxer Revolution in China.

500 grams deboned, skinned pike, 600 grams veal kidney fat, salt, pepper, nutmeg, some lemon juice, 4 egg yolks, 75 milliliters milk.

The pike and kidney fat used to be finely chopped and pestled. Today we run it twice, if necessary, through the finest blade of a food chopper and season with salt, pepper, nutmeg, and lemon juice. Boil the milk, then stir in the egg yolks until it becomes creamy. Fold this mixture into the ground pike mixture. Combine well, then remove from heat. Form into dumplings or use a soup spoon to make quenelles which are then poached in boiling salted water for 15 minutes with some pimiento, bay leaf, a dash of wine vinegar, and ½ onion. Serve with crayfish sauce, garnished with the crayfish tails. Top with chopped parsley and dill and accompany with rice or buttered boiled potatoes, and fresh salads.

Sautéed Pike Perch with Potato Salad

Pike perch has always been very popular in the Berlin area. It was abundant in the surrounding rivers and lakes. This fish is a predator. Young pike perch used to be sautéed whole with the heads, slashed on both sides like young river pike. Larger pike perch is cut into fillets.

1200 grams cleaned and scaled pike perch, salt, pepper, 2 lemons, some flour, 100 grams butter, chopped parsley, 1200 grams peeled boiled potatoes, 2 tablespoons wine vinegar, 100 grams lean bacon, 1 large onion.

Slice the boiled potatoes. Make a marinade using vinegar, some salt, pepper, a dash of sugar, and the diced onion. Boil for 5 minutes. Pour the marinade over the potatoes, then mix in the fried bacon cubes.

Sprinkle the cleaned pike perch with lemon. Season with salt and freshly ground pepper. Roll in flour and sauté in foaming butter, turning frequently until golden brown.

Sprinkle with parsley. Serve with lemon wedges and lettuce on the side.

Carp in Beer Sauce

2 kilograms live carp, 1 large onion, 100 grams celery root, 100 grams dry gingerbread crumbs, ¾ liter beer, a dash of salt, a dash of sugar, 1 lemon, 100 grams butter, 30 grams flour.

Kill, clean, and scale the carp. Cut into fillets, salt and pepper lightly, and sprinkle with lemon juice.

Dice onion and celery.

Dust the fillets lightly with flour. Turning frequently, sauté lightly in butter, then add onion and celery, sauté briefly. Add the gingerbread crumbs and pour in the beer. Cover, and braise slowly. Carefully remove carp pieces from pan, set aside and keep warm. Mix the butter with the flour and bind the carp stock to the desired thickness. Season to taste with salt, pepper, and sugar.

Pour the sauce over the carp and serve.

Serve with buttered boiled potatoes and lettuce.

Green Eel with Cucumber Salad and Buttered Potatoes

1200 grams cleaned eel, salt, pepper, sugar, sage leaves, vinegar, 2 lemons, 80 grams butter, 50 grams flour, 2 egg yolks, ¼ liter cream, 1 large or 2 small cucumbers, parsley, fresh dill, 800 grams potatoes, 1 onion.

Bring water to a boil and add salt, a shot of vinegar, and sage leaves. Add eels and cook until tender for 15–20 minutes. Cut the eel into 150-gram pieces before cooking.

Make a roux using 50 grams butter and the flour. Pour in the eel stock through a strainer. Stir rapidly with a whisk until smooth. Mix the cream with the egg yolks, stir into the eel sauce and remove from heat. Season with lemon juice, salt, pepper, and a dash of sugar.

Stir in the chopped parsley and dill shortly before serving in order to retain the fresh, green color.

Keep the eel pieces warm in the remaining liquid. Meanwhile, the boiled potatoes have been cooked and tossed in melted butter and parsley shortly before serving.

For the salad cut the peeled cucumbers in thin slices, salt lightly. Sprinkle with pepper and sugar as well as diced onion. Add a shot of vinegar, chopped parsley and dill. Mix well, let draw, and, if desired, enhance with cream. Taste before serving.

The flavor should be mildly sweet-sour.

Arrange the skinned eel on plates and cover with the fresh dill sauce. Serve the potatoes separately, the cucumber salad on glass plates.

Serve with a dry white wine!

Crayfish in Dill Sauce

48 crayfish, 100 grams root vegetables (leek, carrots, celery), 1 bunch fresh dill, 1 onion, 2 lemons, ¼ liter sweet cream, 4 egg yolks, 50 grams butter, 50 grams flour, 3 tablespoons vinegar, salt, pepper, sugar, chopped dill, chopped parsley.

Cut the vegetables in small pieces and add to a large pot of water with the dill and peeled onion. Bring to a boil, add vinegar and then the crayfish one by one. Simmer for approx. 15 minutes. Remove from heat and take out crayfish with a skimmer. Rinse quickly under cold water. Pull tail to remove stomach and intestinal vein. Strain the stock and make a roux with butter and flour. Stir in hot crayfish stock with a whisk to the desired thickness. Simmer gently for 10 minutes. Season with salt, pepper, a dash of sugar, and lemon juice. Beat the egg yolks with the cream and mix into the sauce. Remove from heat and stir in dill. If you wish, make crayfish butter with the shells. Dry the warm crayfish tails, cover with dill sauce, dot with crayfish butter, and top with chopped parsley. Serve with rice and green salad.

Poached Cod with Mustard Butter

Around 1790, this fish enjoyed more popularity than the local pike perch. Today, however, pike perch is expensive and scarce.

Those who still remember the old central market hall on Alexanderplatz may become nostalgic thinking about the abundance as well as the prices of fish offered there daily. During the 1920's, a pound of pike-perch came to about 25 pfennigs. Fried, young carp were a delicacy rarely found anymore today.

1500 grams cod, 4 tablespoons vinegar, 1 onion, 1 bay leaf, 4 pimientos, salt, 150 grams butter, 50 grams mustard, 1 lemon.

Clean the cod and take out the inner, black skin. Remove the blood line under the back bone, scale, cut off the fins, and rinse well. Cut into 4 portions.

Bring to a boil 1 liter of water with vinegar, salt, the peeled onion, and the spices. Add the cod portions, bring to a boil again and immediately remove from heat. Let the fish draw for approx. 10 minutes.

Melt the butter in a saucepan. As soon as it begins to brown, stir in a spoonful of mustard.

Accompany the fish with hot boiled potatoes and pour the hot mustard butter over the fish portions. Arrange lemon wedges on a lettuce leaf. Serve with lettuce.

This fish is also good with mustard sauce, in which case you use the fish stock to make a bound mustard sauce to cover the fish.

Blue Tench

4 350- to 400-gram tench, 200 grams butter, 4 table-spoons vinegar, 1 lemon, 1 onion, 1 bay leaf, 4 pimientos, salt, 40 grams grated horseradish, some whipped cream.

Kill the tench with a blow to the head. Clean and wash.

In a pot or fish cooker boil 2 liters of water with vinegar, salt, the peeled onion, and spices.

As in the tench in dill sauce recipe, break the backbones before carefully sliding the fish, one by one, into the boiling water. Simmer for approx. 15 minutes at moderate heat. The fish is done, when the fins can be easily pulled out.

Melt the butter and pour into a sauce boat.

Drain the fish and brush the blue skin with butter so it keeps its blue color. Flourish with parsley (stick a bunch of parsley in the mouth), serve with lemon wedges on a lettuce leaf, boiled potatoes, and cream mixed with horseradish. Gentlemen sometimes prefer brown instead of melted butter.

Blue trout is prepared in the same manner.

Tench in Dill Sauce

4 350- to 400-gram tench, 1 onion, 1 bay leaf, 4 pimientos, a dash of thyme, salt, vinegar, ¼ liter light beef broth, a shot of white wine, 50 grams butter, 40 grams flour, 4 tablespoons sour cream, lemon juice, pepper, sugar, 2 egg yolks, 2 bunches dillweed.

Boil 1½ liters water with salt, 3 tablespoons vinegar, bay leaf, pimientos, thyme and some dillweed.

Kill, clean, and wash the fish. Break the backbones by pressing your thumbs down on the middle of the backbone from top to bottom. This is done to prevent scalding from the flipping of the tail.

Hold the fish's head first in the boiling water before letting them slide slowly into the pot. Simmer slowly until the fish is done, i. e., when the fins can be pulled out easily.

Make a light roux with the butter and flour. Add the beef broth and stir with a whisk until smooth. Add some fish stock. Simmer for 10 minutes, then add the egg yolks mixed with cream. Season to taste with salt, a dash of pepper, sugar, and lemon juice. At the last moment, blend in the chopped dill and a small shot of white wine.

Place the well-drained fish on a plate, pull off the blue skin, and cover with the dill sauce. Serve with lemon wedges on lettuce leaves. Accompany with green salad and buttered boiled potatoes.

71

Notes and more recipes

Notes and more recipes

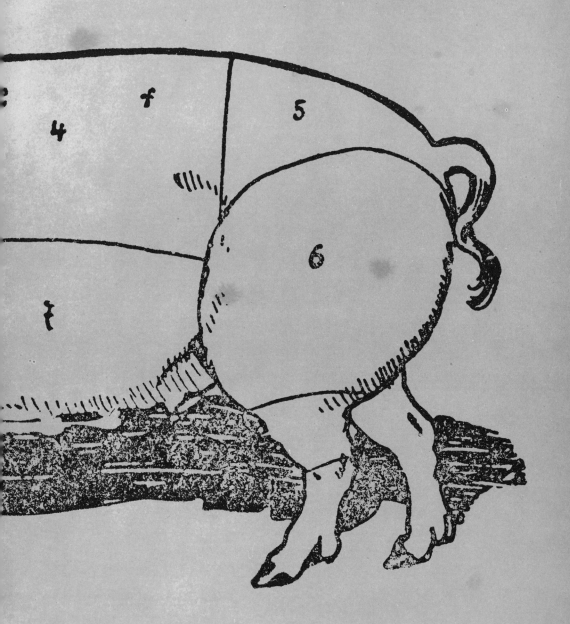

Meat Patties

Meat patties are a favorite staple food in Berlin. They are eaten as a quick snack on the way out the door, at pubs, and on any other occasion. They even appear at rustic buffets next to the famous raw ground beef sandwiches. They are good, cold or warm, with beer, a roll, and, of course, mustard.

Naturally the patties also contain bread inside of them, but only in moderate amounts.

125 grams ground beef, 125 grams ground pork, 125 grams ground veal, 125 grams fine sausage meat, 50 grams butter, 2 rolls, approx. 1 cup milk, salt, pepper, a dash of nutmeg.

Soak the rolls in milk, squeeze out liquid, and mix with the meat and spices until well combined.

Form into equal-sized flat patties and brown lightly on both sides in the hot butter.

This is the best meat patty recipe, a favorite of Berlin butchers.

Pigs' Knuckles

This is a true Berlin classic served on almost any occasion, especially during winter.

This dish first appeared in the 19th century in a restaurant near the old Görlitz train station, where the trains came in from Niederlausitz, Silisia, and Oderbruch.

It is said that patrons from the country passed on the recipe to a Berlin restaurant owner. For farmers in particular, pickling was then the most common way of preserving food, as modern refrigeration did not yet exist.

2000–2400 grams pigs' knuckles, pickled and cut by the butcher into 500- to 600-gram portions, 5 pimientos, 4 peppercorns, 2 bay leaves, 1 onion, a dash of sugar.

Clean the knuckles well and place in a large pot with 3 liters water, the spices, and the peeled onion. Simmer gently until tender, for approx. 1 hour.

Check the meat with your thumb. The meat is done if it comes off the bone easily. Adding a dash of sugar while the knuckles are simmering will give the meat a marzipan-pink color. Serve on plates or porcelain platters with puréed yellow peas, sauerkraut, and two boiled potato halves. Top the purée with a spoonful of panache (fried bacon and onion cubes). Place a variety of mustards on the table and don't forget the beer.

Casseler Spare-Ribs

This dish was invented in the 19th century by a Berlin butcher on Potsdamer Strasse named Cassel.

> *800 grams spare-ribs (1 rack), ½ liter water, 1 large carrot, 1 medium-sized onion, 1 bay leaf, 5 juniper berries, a healthy shot of red wine, ⅛ liter sour cream, approx. 1 teaspoon cornstarch, some freshly ground pepper.*

Rinse ribs and place on an oven pan with the fatty side down. Add the peeled, coarsely chopped onion, carrot slices, bay leaf, crushed peppercorns, and juniper berries. Douse with the ½ liter boiling water and bake in a preheated oven at moderate heat.

Turn the ribs over after a half an hour. Bake another 40 minutes, basting frequently. Add water, if necessary.

When ribs are done, remove from oven and take the meat off the bones with a short boning knife. Cover the meat and keep warm. Break up the bones and replace in the pan.

Strain the meat stock. Boil quickly with the red wine. Mix some cornstarch with the sour cream and bind the sauce with the mixture. Add pepper and, if necessary, season with salt.

Slice the meat and cover with sauce. Serve extra sauce on the side. Sauerkraut, red cabbage, and spinach are excellent side dishes.

Meat Loaf with Cream Sauce

500 grams lean, finely ground meat (half beef, half pork), 1 soaked stale roll, 50 grams finely diced onions, 1 egg, salt, pepper, nutmeg, juice of ½ lemon, 100 grams fatty bacon, 50 grams lard, 1 teaspoon flour, 1 cup sour cream.

Mix well the ground meat with the egg, drained roll, salt, pepper, dash of nutmeg, and diced bacon.

With wet hands, form a bread-shaped loaf.

Heat the lard in an oven pan and place the meat loaf in it. Bake in a moderate oven for approx. half an hour, basting frequently until brown. Remove from oven when done.

Now pour the fat out of the pan and add a half cup of water. Boil thoroughly, then add the sour cream.

Make a roux with some of the drained fat and flour, and bind the sauce to the desired thickness.

Season to taste with salt, pepper, and lemon juice.

To serve, cut into slices and pour over the sauce. Good with – depending on the season – red cabbage, kale, spinach, green beans, boiled or mashed potatoes.

Ragout Fin

Like so many other things, the Huguenots brought ragout fin to Berlin. Here the dish became famous, not in France.

125 grams boiled veal, 125 grams boiled chicken, 1 pair small calf sweetbreads, 1 boiled veal tongue, 125 grams cooked mushrooms, 50–60 grams butter, 40 grams flour, 1 cup each veal and chicken broth, some milk, ¼ cup white wine, ½ cup sweet cream, 2 egg yolks, juice of ½ lemon, salt, pepper, sugar, a shot of Worcester sauce, 40–50 grams grated parmesan cheese.

78

On the day before, boil the chicken, veal, and veal tongue in salted water with onion, 2 pimientos, and 1 bay leaf.

Poach the sweetbreads in salted water with a small shot of vinegar. Skin the tongue and the sweetbreads. Cut the meat, tongue, sweetbreads, and mushrooms into bite-sized pieces.

Make a light roux with the flour and butter. Stir in the hot stock and some milk until smooth. Simmer slowly for 15 minutes, add the wine. If the sauce is too thick, add more stock; if too thin, bind again. Season with salt, pepper, a dash of sugar, lemon juice, and a few drops of Worcester sauce. Mix the egg yolks with the cream, remove the sauce from the heat and stir in the egg/cream mixture. Now add the diced meat, stir well, and season to taste if necessary.

The sauce should bind and cover well as the ragout should not be runny. Pour into 4 St. Jacques shells, sprinkle with parmesan, dot with butter, and place in a hot oven or grill for a few minutes until golden brown.

Serve with lemon wedges.

Fresh Blood Sausage and Liverwurst *Love it!*

This is an old Berlin dish that has steadfastly held its own. The restaurant best known for upholding this tradition is Hardtke on Meineckestrasse near the Ku'damm. High-ranking politicians and celebrities always tried this hearty meal during their stay in Berlin, accompanied, of course, by a "Molle" (beer) and followed by a few "Körner" (corn schnapps).

At the end of the 18th century, 188 years ago, a pub owner named Friebel inadvertently started the custom by standing outside of his bistro at Molkenmarkt 11 on Fridays – the slaughter day – after a day's work, in a lily-white apron. This was the signal for the people in the area that the work was now finished. His pub then quickly filled with people eager to eat sausage soup or fresh blood sausage and liverwurst. Soon other restaurateurs imitated him.

Today, instead of the white apron, a white flag is hung outside of the establishment with the inscription: Today Fresh Blood Sausage and Liverwurst.

From your butcher, buy 1 fresh blood and 1 liver sausage per person.

After heating, the sausages should not be runny, but also not too firm. Their tasty inside should spill out of the casings after cutting.

Serve with sauerkraut and boiled potatoes, or, if you 're not too hungry, a roll.

There is also the "Schlachtplatte", which includes, in addition to the sausages and sauerkraut, a slice of boiled pork, a piece of boiled pork kidney, a liver dumpling, and, if possible, a grilled sausage.

Naturally, a variety of mustards is a must.

Gänseklein with Parsley Sauce

This dish has always been a particular favorite at Christmas. In the olden days, of course, the goose came from the area, not out of the freezer.

Mother, after careful inspection, bought the goose from one of the many venison and poultry merchants. The children would watch curiously while she picked, cleaned, and singed the goose in the kitchen. The Gänseklein was prepared with the wings, heart, gizzard, head, neck, and feet, and served one or two days before Christmas eve. This meal represented the start of holiday festivities.

Use the neck, head, wings, feet, stomach, and heart of the goose.
50 grams butter, 45 grams flour, ½ cup sweet cream, 4 peppercorns, 4 pimientos, 1 bay leaf, 1 carrot, 140 grams celery root, 1 parsley root, ½ leek stalk, salt, a dash of sugar, juice of ½ lemon, 1 large bunch curly parsley.

Singe the head, neck, and wings. Chop the beak off the head, remove the claws from the feet. Pull the gullet out of the neck. Boil the feet and stomach and pull off the skin.

Drain well and clean. Replace in boiling water, drain, and rinse with cold water. Place in cold water with a bit of salt. When it boils, skim off the scum, then add the spices and the soup greens. Simmer until the meat is tender, but not so tender that it falls apart. Strain the stock. Keep the meat warm.

Mix the butter with flour and add enough stock to thicken. Simmer and stir for 10 minutes, then add the cream. Season with salt, pepper, lemon juice, and sugar. Finish off with the freshly chopped parsley.

Pour the gravy over the meat and serve with buttered rice or boiled potatoes.

Pickled Goose Legs

2 large or 3 small goose legs, 1 onion, 1 bay leaf, 4 pi-mientos, 50 grams salt, 6 grams sugar, 8 grams pickling salt.

Boil 1½ liters water with salt, sugar, and pickling salt. Let cool, then add the goose legs with the peeled onion, bay leaf, and pimientos. Pickle for 3 days.

Place the pickled goose legs in boiling water, cover, and simmer for approx. 1½ hours.

Cut the legs in half and serve with Teltower turnips and boiled potatoes.

Roast Goose

The Berliners have always loved poultry. After the war, chicken became especially popular, thanks to "Hühner-Hugo" (Chicken Hugo). Goose, however, has always been in first place, especially at Christmas. The geese from Oderbruch are the preferred type of these domesticated birds. Berlin has always been the trade center for this fowl in central Europe.

1 young, 3-kilogram goose, 2 cleaned, cored apples, 1 bunch dried mugwort, salt.

Draw and singe the goose. Cut off the neck, and chop off the feet below the joint. Clean well and chop off the wings. Reserve the stomach, heart, wings, neck, and feet for Gänseklein. For serving at home, it is not necessary to secure the goose with thread. Rub the goose inside and out with salt. Stick the legs into the stomach pockets on the sides. Stuff with the apples and the mugwort and sew up the opening with thread. Place the goose on a rack, breast down, in a pan with a bit of water and place in a preheated moderate oven.

Turn the goose every 15–20 minutes, basting frequently with the juices. This is very important.

If necessary, pour off the fat with a small ladle. For the gravy, it is important to add water when the sediment is still brown. If you wait too long it will turn black and taste bitter. Do not, however, add the water too soon, to assure, that the right aromas are released and that the sauce retains its nice brown color.

The right time to add water is when the sediment foams up when the water is poured in. It is advisable, at this time, to loosen the sediment on the sides of the pan, to retain these roasting flavors as well.

The more often you reduce and add water, the better the sauce will be in color and flavor.

The roasting time for young geese is approx. 2 hours, for older geese, 3½ hours. Turn the goose on its back towards the end of the roasting time, so that the breast skin achieves the desired and beloved crispiness. You can tell if the goose is done by pressing the legs with your thumbs: if you can easily press down to the leg bones, the goose is ready.

Remove goose from pan and cut in half lengthwise. Remove the mugwort and put the apples aside.

Remove, as best you can, bones, breastplate and ribs. Replace in pan and return to oven. Take slices from the breast piece, middle piece, and leg from each half, set aside and keep warm.

Dust the remaining reduced brown drippings in the pan with a bit of flour – not too much – and cover with water. Boil thoroughly for 10 minutes, strain, and serve separately with the goose.

The Berliner accompanies his favorite dish with red cabbage, kale and potatoes, or Silesian dumplings. The apples are served alongside the meat.

Invite Auntie Helga

Green Beans and Lamb

1 kilogram lamb ribs, 2 onions, 800 grams potatoes, 800 grams green beans, 50 grams lean bacon, 30 grams flour, 1 bay leaf, 1 pimiento, 1 clove, salt, pepper, savory, parsley.

Bring a pot of water to a boil. Remove the extra fat from the ribs and add to the water with the bay leaf, pimiento, clove, and 1 whole onion. Simmer gently until tender.

Cut the bacon in squares and sauté lightly with the diced onion. Make a roux with the flour and bind the beans with it.

Season the beans to taste with salt, pepper, and crumbled summer savory.

Serve the beans on a flat plate or oval porcelain platter and place pieces of the hot, boiled rips on top. Sprinkle with chopped parsley and arrange two or three boiled potatoes around the edge of the plate.

Berlin Chicken Fricassee

This is the original recipe which, as you can see, is rather lavish in the time and ingredients required. Before the last war, this dish was prepared in this way in every respectable household – unbelievable for our circumstances today.

1 1-kilogram stewing chicken, 1 small pair calf sweetbreads, 1 small calf tongue, approx. 250 grams cow udder, 150 grams raw, cleaned mushrooms, 125 grams cleaned morels, 12 asparagus spears, 12 crayfish tails, 12 very small semolina dumplings, 4 crayfish shells filled with semolina mixture, 4 pâte brisée crescents, 1 carrot, 100 grams cleaned celery root, 1 onion, 4 peppercorns, 4 pimientos, 1 bay leaf, ½ cup white wine, salt, pepper, juice of ½ lemon and some of the peel, ¾ cup sweet cream, 2 egg yolks, 50 grams butter, 45 grams flour, 1 pinch of sugar, a shake of Worcester sauce.

The cow udder should best be boiled on the day before and left to cool in the stock.

Boil the chicken in a stewing pan with plenty of water, together with the salt and spices. After it comes to a boil, remove scum. Then add the root vegetables and simmer, depending on the age of the chicken, for 2–2½ hours. The calf tongue and sweetbreads are cooked separately in salted water. When the sweetbreads are thoroughly boiled, after approx. 15 minutes, remove from pot, rinse with cold water, trim, and set aside. When the calf tongue is tender, also rinse with cold water and skin. The chicken should be tender but not falling apart. Debone and cut meat into bite-sized pieces. Meanwhile, steam the mushrooms, the morels, and the asparagus spears separately in small saucepans.

Make a semolina batter with milk, egg, salt, and nutmeg. Form 12 small semolina dumplings and cook in gently boiling salted water together with the 4 semolina stuffed crayfish shells.

Now take about ½ liter of the strained chicken broth and add the white wine, some mushroom liquid, morel liquid, and tongue broth.

Make a roux with the butter and flour, stirring constantly with a whisk until the desired thickness is achieved. Simmer gently for 15 minutes with a piece of lemon peel. Season with salt, pepper, a dash of sugar, lemon juice, and a shake of Worcester sauce. Stir in the cream/egg yolk mixture and remove from heat. Pour through a strainer.

Proceed as follows with the other ingredients, which have been kept warm:

Arrange the chicken meat in a deep dish, then layer with calf tongue, cow udder, sweetbreads, morels, mushrooms, crayfish tails, and asparagus spears. Cover everything with hot sauce and serve the rest of the sauce separately in a gravy boat.

Arrange the semolina dumplings, pâte brisée crescents, and crayfish shells around the edge of the dish. If available, sprinkle with melted crayfish butter, place capers in the center, and top with chopped parsley.

Serve with buttered rice.

As fresh morels are relatively scarce, you may use canned ones.

Even if you leave out the crayfish, you'll still have a typical Berlin dish.

Berlin Zwiebelfleisch

It is great-granddad's favorite dish of old Berlin.

800 grams lean mutton from the shoulder or neck, 800 grams peeled onions, approx. 5 grams caraway seeds, salt, pepper, 40–50 grams flour.

Cut the meat into bite-sized ragout pieces. Halve the onions and slice. Place the meat and onions in a deep pot and just cover with water. Add some salt and bring to a boil. Remove the scum and then add the caraway seeds. Simmer gently until the meat is tender. Bind with a flour and water mixture. Simmer a few more minutes. Taste, and season if necessary. Serve with boiled potatoes and a beer.

Roasted Veal Brisket with Gooseberries

This was the all-time favorite of our revered "prince among poets," Theodor Fontane. It is truly a historical meal. Fontane's grandmother created this dish for her grandson. The recipe spread by word of mouth through Berlin by cooks and into middle-class kitchens.

Since then the recipe has been largely forgotten.

1 kilogram veal brisket, 45 grams butter, salt, pepper, pinch of cinnamon, some grated lemon peel, 25 grams sugar, 300 grams unripe gooseberries, 3–4 egg yolks, ½ cup white wine.

Rub the brisket with salt and pepper and bake in a greased roasting pan. Turn and baste occasionally until both sides are nice and brown.

Add the washed and cleaned gooseberries and a dash of grated lemon peel. Once they are steamed, add the cinnamon and sugar, then add the white wine.

Braise the brisket in the developing pan juices at moderate heat until tender. Add water to pan if necessary.

When the meat is done, set it aside, keep warm, and strain the pan juices. Bind the sauce with the beaten egg yolks only.

Serve together with mashed potatoes, preferably prepared the old-fashioned way, then you'll have a real historical dish.

Berlin Veal Fricassee

This is the original Berlin recipe.

> *1 kilogram lean calf brisket, 1 small pair calf sweet-breads, 200 grams morels, ½ cauliflower, some asparagus pieces, 50 grams capers, 1 onion, 100 grams celery root, 3 peppercorns, 1 bay leaf, 1 small glass white wine, ½ cup sweet cream, 2 egg yolks, ½ lemon, 50 grams butter, 45 grams flour, salt, pepper, sugar, some Worcester sauce for seasoning.*

Cut the calf brisket into bite-sized ragout pieces. Place in a saucepan with hot water and some salt. Bring to a boil and remove the scum.

Add the root vegetables and spices. Simmer gently until tender, for approx. ¾–1 hour. Strain the stock, cover the meat and keep warm.

Poach the soaked sweetbreads until very tender. Trim and reserve. Thoroughly boil the cauliflower florets and set aside. Do the same with the morels and asparagus pieces.

Prepare a roux with the butter and flour, stirring constantly, adding the white wine and as much of the stock as necessary. Cook with a piece of lemon peel for 15 minutes. Then season with salt, a dash of pepper, and sugar, lemon juice, and a few drops of Worcester sauce. Fold in the egg yolks mixed with cream, then pass the sauce through the strainer.

Arrange the drained fricassee meat in a bowl and cover with a layer of the sliced sweetbreads, cauliflower florets, morels, and asparagus pieces. Pour over the fricassee sauce and sprinkle with capers.

Serve with buttered rice, such as Bali rice. *Max fixed this for us*

87

Berlin Calf Liver

700 grams calf liver, 200 grams peeled onions, 12 cored apple slices, 80 grams butter, some flour for coating, some chopped parsley, salt, pepper.

Remove the outer skin and veins. Cut the liver into medium-sized slices, season with salt and pepper, coat lightly with flour, and brown lightly on both sides in butter, leaving the inside pink. In a separate skillet sauté the apple slices (approx. 1 cm thick) and thinly sliced onions until golden.

Serve the sautéed liver on plates or a platter. Cover with the onions, then the apple slices, and top with chopped parsley.

For a nice visual effect, you may place a steamed cherry in the center of each apple slice.

Accompany with apple sauce and salad.

Stuffed Cabbage Rolls

This is traditional, basic fare – also a favorite of housewives as it is relatively inexpensive. When cabbage rolls are for dinner, young and old hurry to the table.

750 grams lean ground meat (half beef, half pork), 1 soaked stale roll, 1 small onion, 1 egg, salt, pepper, nutmeg, 800 grams white cabbage, 4 nice slices of smoked lean bacon, salt, pepper, caraway seeds, 1 carrot, 100 grams cleaned celery root, 1 onion, some small pieces of bacon rind, 1 tablespoon flour.

Mix the meat with the drained roll, diced onion, salt, pepper, nutmeg, and egg. Cut the stem from the cabbage and clean. Blanch the large leaves in boiling water for about 10 minutes, then rinse with cold water and place on a cloth or colander to dry. Spread the cabbage leaves in 4 equal portions on the kitchen table, sprinkle with salt, pepper, and caraway seeds. Place equal portions of the meat on each leaf. Roll the meat up in the leaves and tie with a thin thread.

Meanwhile, put the diced carrot, celery, onion, and bacon rind in a roasting pan in the oven. When it is hot, remove from oven, add the cabbage rolls and place a slice of bacon on top of each one. Place the cabbage rolls in a hot oven until they acquire some color. Add water. When the cabbage rolls are tender (test with your thumb), remove and set aside to keep warm. Strain the juices, add some water and stir in the flour for the desired thickness. Serve with the cabbage rolls. Accompany with boiled potatoes. You may wish to enhance the sauce with sour cream.

Grandma's recipe

Königsberger Klopse

This dish originated in East Prussia, proving yet again the openness of the old capital of Germany to regional influences.

> *600 grams finely ground meat (half beef, half pork), 1 soaked stale roll, approx. 50 grams diced onion, pimientos, 1 bay leaf, 50 grams butter, 40–50 grams flour, 4 drained anchovies, 50 grams capers, juice of ½ lemon, salt, pepper, a dash of sugar, 1 teaspoon Worcester sauce, ½ cup sweet cream, 1–2 egg yolks, 1 whole egg.*

Drain the roll and mix with the meat, onion, and the whole egg. Season with salt and pepper. Combine well. Shape into approx. 75-gram round balls and drop these into salted boiling water with some pimiento and the bay leaf. Simmer about 20 minutes.

Make a light roux with the butter and flour. Add stock as necessary to thicken and stir with a whisk until smooth.

Cook for 10–15 minutes over moderate heat, stirring with a wooden spoon. Season to taste with salt, pepper, sugar, lemon juice, and Worcester sauce. Stir in capers and finish off with the egg yolks beaten with the cream. Remove from heat.

Pour the gravy over the meatballs and serve with boiled potatoes, pickles, mustard pickles, or red beets.

Lung Hash with Fried Eggs

1 calf lung, 1 calf heart, 1 onion, 1 carrot, 1 parsley root, 100 grams celery root, 5 pimientos, 1 bay leaf. For the sauce: 50 grams butter, 50 grams flour, 50 grams diced onion, salt, pepper, a dash of sugar, some vinegar, 1 kosher pickle, 4 eggs.

Wash and clean the lung and heart well. Cut into pieces and bring to a boil in salted water. Remove the scum and add the root vegetables and spices. Cover and simmer gently until tender, for approx. 1¾ hours.

Sauté the diced onion in butter until transparent, add the flour and prepare a light roux. Stirring constantly with a whisk, add enough of the meat stock to make a thick sauce. Simmer for 10 more minutes. Put the cooled meat through a meat grinder set at medium, and bind with the sauce. Season with salt, pepper, vinegar, and sugar.

Serve with a fried egg, a few kosher pickle slices, and boiled potatoes.

Pökelkamm

Pökelkamm is a pigs' neck. Along with pigs' knuckles, it is one of Berlin's favorite winter dishes.

900 grams pickled pig's neck, 1 onion, 1 bay leaf, 4 pimientos, a dash of sugar.

Remove bones before cooking, if possible.

Bring to a boil approx. 1½ liters water with the onion, spices, and sugar. Add the meat, cover, and simmer for approx. 1 hour until tender.

Remove from pot, cut into approx. 1½ centimeters thick slices. Pour some stock over the meat and accompany with, as with pigs' knuckles, sauerkraut, purée of peas with bacon and onions, and a few boiled potatoes.

Braised Pig's Neck

1 kilogram fresh pig's neck, 100 grams root vegetables (carrots, celery, leeks), 1 onion, 1 teaspoon caraway seeds, 1 bay leaf, 4 pimientos, 4 juniper berries, 40 grams flour, salt, pepper.

Remove bones and chop meat into small pieces. Rub the meat with salt and pepper. Place in a roasting pan with ¼ liter water and place in a preheated oven. Turn and baste frequently with the pan juices. As soon as the juices are reduced, add the finely chopped vegetables and sliced onion. Stir frequently.

It is advisable to add approx. 5 grams tomato paste to give the sauce a nice brown color. Add more water and braise until the meat is tender. Bind the sauce with a bit of flour, and season to taste with salt and pepper. Strain and pour over the meat. Good accompaniments are red cabbage, Teltower turnips, spinach, steamed cucumbers, potatoes, pea purée, and dumplings.

Pork Belly

In Berlin, pork belly is preferred boiled.

800 grams lean pork belly, 1 bay leaf, 5 pimientos, 1 tablespoon caraway seeds, 4 crushed peppercorns, salt, 1 onion, 1 piece bacon or bacon rind, 1 kilogram sauerkraut, ⅛ liter cream, salt, a dash of sugar, 1 grated potato.

Slit the skin around the ribs with a knife so that the bones can be removed when the meat is done.

Bring to a boil, 1½ liters water with the bay leaf, pimientos, caraway seeds, peppercorns, peeled onion, and bacon rind. Add some salt, the shredded sauerkraut and the pork belly. Cover and simmer until tender for approx. 50 minutes. Remove the bay leaf, onion, and pork belly. Cut the pork belly in slices and reserve.

Mix the cream with the grated potato and combine with the sauerkraut. Season with salt and sugar.

Serve the meat on a bed of sauerkraut and accompany with boiled potatoes.

Stuffed Beef Rolls with Mashed Potatoes and Red Cabbage

This is a common and popular Berlin Sunday dinner.

> 4   180-gram strips (thin) pounded round or flank steak, 1 large onion, 4 thick strips bacon, 4 slices sour pickle, approx. 20 grams mustard, 25 grams butter, 60 grams lard, ½ cup sweet cream, some potato flour, salt, pepper.

Slice the onion and sauté in butter until transparent. Spread the meat strips on the table, pound if necessary, season with salt and pepper, brush with mustard. Spread the sautéed onion evenly on the strips and top with a slice of pickle and a strip of bacon. Now roll meat and tie with thread or secure with a toothpick.

Brown the meat rolls on all sides in hot lard in a cast-iron pan. Then fill the pan half full with water, cover, and, if possible, braise in the oven until tender. This should take approx. 2 hours. When the meat is done, remove from pan, set aside, and keep warm. Quickly add the cream to the pan juices, bring to a boil, and bind lightly with some potato flour.

Season to taste with salt and pepper.

Remove threads or toothpicks before serving.

Red cabbage and mashed potatoes are an especially good accompaniment.

Beef Brisket with Bouillon Potatoes, Horseradish Sauce, and Red Beets

This is one of Berlin's heartiest dishes.

> 1 kilogram fresh deboned beef brisket, 1 carrot, ½ leek stalk, 150 grams celery root, 1 parsley root, 50 grams butter, 40 grams flour, 70 grams freshly grated horseradish, ½ cup sweet cream, salt, pepper, a dash of sugar, juice of ½ lemon, 3 pimientos, 1 bay leaf.

Place the beef brisket in 1 liter water with some salt, the pimientos, the bay leaf, and the chopped root vegetables. Bring to a boil. Remove the scum and simmer gently until tender for about 2–2½ hours. Remove the meat and keep warm. Strain the stock and keep warm.

Prepare a light roux with the flour and butter. Stirring constantly, add stock until the sauce has the desired thickness. Simmer gently for approx. 10 minutes, then add the cream and the grated horseradish. Season to taste with salt, pepper, sugar, and lemon juice.

Cut the beef brisket into medium-sized portions and serve covered with horseradish sauce. Accompany with bouillon potatoes (recipe in this book) and red beets, kosher or mustard pickles.

You may bind the horseradish sauce simply with soaked white bread instead of flour. It is also customary to use pickled instead of fresh beef brisket.

Prussian Tripe

Königsberg, in East Prussia, was Frederick the Great's favorite territory. Our great thinker Kant presided there as well as Frederick's Infantry Regiment No. 1, signifying the importance of this Prussian territory.

This dish undoubtedly came to the old German capital via Königsberg.

Many tripe restaurants, especially those near the harbor, opened their doors at dawn already, before the first cockcrow. The first guests to come in out of the icy east-north-east-wind whistling through the streets included dockloaders, packers, longshoremen, stevedores, and nightowls. While most people were still in bed, for others the day was just beginning or ending with this meal.

The tripe soup was ladled out of steaming hot kettles, accompanied by a blob of mustard, a dash of ground, dried marjoram, and, for some, a shot of vinegar. This hearty dish got rid of hangovers, and warmed you through and through. It tasted good with a crisp, fresh roll and a beer. Bowls of tripe soup were even sold on the street from vendors' steaming kettles. And here you have the old recipe:

1 kilogram raw beef tripe, 1 kilogram beef marrow bones, 2 celery roots, 1 parsley root, 2 onions, 1 carrot, 6 pimientos, 10 peppercorns, 2 bay leaves, vinegar, 2 tablespoons dried, ground marjoram.

Begin preparation the day before. Wash the tripe well and cut into large pieces. Place in a deep pot with the bones and cover with water and a bit of salt. Simmer gently for approx. 3½ hours. Then add the chopped celery and parsley roots, onions, carrot as well as the spices and simmer for another half an hour. Test for tenderness, if not ready, cook for another half an hour.

Remove the marrow bones and the tripe pieces. After the tripe has cooled somewhat, cut into strips or squares and replace in soup. Then add a shot of vinegar and the marjoram. The soup shoud be thick, but it is not usually bound with flour.

Serve very hot.

Holstein Schnitzel

There are many stories surrounding this dish, but it definitely has nothing to do with the province of Schleswig-Holstein. Its name stems from the "eminence grise," privy councillor Fritz von Holstein. He was a member of Bismarck's cabinet, and used to frequent the wine restaurant F. W. Borchardt, on Französische Strasse near Unter den Linden. Holstein was not a leisurely gourmet. He was taciturn, but managed to ask the waiter for "mein Schnitzel."

My father, chef Fritz Becker Sr., learned his trade from a royal restaurateur and later became chef at the restaurant "Unter den Linden," just a step away from F. W. Borchardt. He and Director Willmer from the nearby "Kempinski" restaurant heard the story of this dish first hand from an F. W. Borchardt chef.

One day the privy councillor again hastily ordered "mein Schnitzel" and an appetizer. Whether on purpose or simply because of the pressure and pace in the kitchen, the following new dish was born. Although it has survived over the years, it is often prepared incorrectly.

F. W. Borchardt's waiter served it as follows:

1 approx. 180-grams veal cutlet seasoned with salt and hand-ground pepper, breaded, sautéed in butter, topped with a fried egg, sprinkled with capers, accompanied by white bread browned in butter and cut in triangles, topped with caviar, smoked salmon, anchovies, sardines, and, as a garnish, red beets and a sour kosher pickle on lettuce leaves.

This really tastes great!

Stolzer Heinrich

This is one of the true ethnic dishes of Berlin, dating back to the era of Queen Luise.

It is also known as Bratwurst in Beer Sauce.

> *4   125-gram sausages (Bratwurst) per person,*
> *50 grams butter, 1 bottle dark beer, 4 pieces ginger-*
> *bread, salt, pepper, a dash of sugar.*

Simmer the sausages beforehand. Puncture on both sides and roll in milk. Then fry in hot butter on both sides until golden brown. Remove from frying pan and keep warm. Now stir the crushed gingerbread in the pan with butter until it dissolves. Pour in the beer, stir, and bring to a boil.

Season with sugar, pepper, and salt. Pour the sauce over the sausages and serve.

In Berlin this dish is accompanied by buttermilk-mashed potatoes with fried diced lean bacon stirred in.

Braised Rabbit Legs in Cream Sauce

> *4 300-gram rabbit legs, 100 grams smoked bacon in*
> *strips, salt, handground pepper.*
> *For the wet marinade:*
> *½ liter red wine, approx. ½ wine glass vinegar,*
> *100 grams root vegetables, garlic, 5 pimientos,*
> *5 peppercorns, 6 juniper berries.*
> *For the sauce:*
> *60 grams lard, leftover bacon bits, 1 small can tomato*
> *paste, salt, pepper, sugar, 50 grams flour, ⅛ liter sour*
> *cream, juice of ½ lemon, 2 tablespoons red wine.*

Clean and skin the rabbit legs. Lard, and leave in the marinade 2–3 days. Remove, pat dry, salt and pepper.

Place the rabbit legs in a preheated, hot oven and sear on all sides in the hot fat. Then add vegetables and bacon bits. Sauté for a few minutes, then douse with water or stock. Reduce and repeat this process twice. Now add ½ liter stock and braise the rabbit legs for 2–2½ hours, turning frequently. Remove the legs and keep warm. Mix the flour with the sour cream, stir into the drippings and thicken. Add tomato paste and simmer slowly for 10 minutes. Season with salt and pepper, a dash of sugar, lemon juice, and red wine. Strain the sauce through a fine sieve and pour over the meat. Serve with red cabbage, kale, Brussels sprouts, apple sauce and cranberries, chestnuts, or mashed potatoes.

The Hobby Gardener's Sunday Roast

1 kilogram rabbit meat (legs and thighs), 1 rabbit liver, butter, ⅛ liter sour cream, 100 grams root vegetables (carrots, leek, celery, parsley root), 40 grams flour, salt, freshly ground pepper, sweet paprika powder, lemon juice.

Wash and dry the meat. Season with salt, pepper, and paprika. In a preheated hot oven, melt butter in roasting pan. Add meat and liver and brown, turning frequently. Add vegetables and sauté briefly. Add water, reduce, and repeat. Then add ⅜ liter water or stock and simmer until done. Test for doneness with your thumb. Remove meat and liver and keep warm. Mix the flour with the cream and fold into the drippings stirring constantly. Simmer slowly for 10 minutes. Season to taste with salt, pepper, and lemon juice. Strain and pour over the meat. Serve with mashed or steamed potatoes, and homegrown cabbage.

Notes and more recipes

To alleviate the game taste, marinate for several days in butter-milk or skim milk. This will also tenderize the meat.

Only connoisseurs of the strong flavor of game prepare the meat without marinating.

Wet marinade:

Is made of 90% good, red cooking wine and 10% vinegar. Add to the marinade coarsely chopped root vegetables; leek, carrots, onions, and celery, 1 bay leaf.

Marinate game for a few days.

Dry marinade:

The skinned, larded game is brushed with oil and covered with thin lemon slices. Sprinkle with crushed juniper berries and herbs and drizzle with a few drops of brandy. Cover and refrigerate for 2 days.

Notes and more recipes

fig · 9

Cold Dishes

Eel in Aspic

Approx. 1300 grams cleaned, fresh eel, 100 grams soup greens, sage leaves, thyme, salt, peppercorns, basil, ½ wine glass vinegar, 2 egg whites, 50–60 grams gelatine.

Rub the eel with salt and rinse with water.

Bring to the boiling point 1½ liters water with salt, herbs, and a dash of vinegar. Drop the sliced eel into the boiling water and simmer slowly until tender for about 20–25 minutes. Remove the eel pieces with a slotted spoon. Stir the slightly beaten egg whites into the stock to clarify, boil again briefly, and remove from heat. Stir in the dissolved gelatine. Let ticken for a while, then strain through a cheese-cloth.

Brush a mold with oil. Place in it the eel pieces and cover with the cooled aspic. Chill, then turn out on a platter decorated with shredded lettuce, boiled egg slices or quarters, salmon rolls, and asparagus spears.

Serve with crunchy, fried potatoes made from boiled potatoes.

Bismarck Herring

This was one of the favorite dishes of the "iron chancellor," Otto von Bismarck. He also enjoyed peewit eggs, the famous Pichelstein stew, and orange ice cream.

He ate the peewit eggs with crayfish ragout in pâte brisée or on creamed morels.

4 large, cleaned, fresh herring, 2 cups vinegar, 1 cup white wine, 1 large, cleaned carrot, 100 grams peeled, sliced onion, 1 kosher pickle, 1 bay leaf, 5 pimientos, 1 tablespoon mustard seed, 1 tablespoon salt, a dash of sugar.

Boil vinegar and white wine with spices, onion slices, and sliced carrot for 10 minutes. Cool.

Add the cleaned, drained herring, and sliced kosher pickle and marinate for approx. 48 hours.

Serve herring covered with pickle and carrot slices, onion rings, and some of the marinade.

In Berlin, Bismarck herring is eaten with rolls or potatoes boiled in their jackets.

It has also become customary to mix some mayonnaise and sweet cream with a bit of the marinade and pour this mixture over the herring.

Fried Herring

Fried herring has always been a favorite snack.

It is jokingly called "worker's trout," although this social stigma will soon disappear, as herring prices slowly but surely move closer to the trout prices.

In Berlin during the twenties, one could still buy 12 herring for 50 pfennigs, which is almost unbelievable today.

Now this "food for the people" costs DM 2.00 per herring.

> *8 large herring, 100 grams flour, 8 onions, 2 bay leaves, 5 pimientos, 50 grams oil, 5 tablespoons vinegar, Worcester sauce, salt, pepper, a dash of sugar.*

Scale and clean the fish. Cut off head, soak, wash, and drain. Season with salt, pepper, vinegar, and a shake of Worcester sauce.

Brown the flour, stirring constantly, in a dry hot skillet. Pour in a deep dish and let cool. Roll the herring in the flour and fry in hot oil until brown on both sides, turning frequently. Add plenty of vinegar to ¼ liter water as well as salt, pepper, sugar, bay leaf, pimiento, and the sliced onion. Boil for 10 minutes. Place the fried herring in this stock for at least 24 hours. Serve with fried potatoes or buttered black bread.

I could eat this every day

Hackepeter

This is a typical Berlin delicacy. It is eaten as a betweenmeal snack, spread on a half a roll with a slice of kosher pickle and diced onion on top.

600 grams medium ground pork (²⁄₃ lean and ¹⁄₃ fatty meat), 1 onion, salt, freshly ground white and black pepper (mixed), 1 teaspoon chopped caraway seeds.

Combine well the ground pork with the spices and finely diced onion. Spread, as described above, on roll halves and serve. In Berlin it is accompanied by a beer and a corn schnapps.

White Jellied Goose

1200 grams goose meat with bones, 1 kilogram calves' feet, 150-gram mixture of celery root, carrots and leek, salt, pepper, vinegar, a dash of sugar, 5–6 egg whites, bunches of parsley and mugwort.

Wash and clean the goose and calves' feet well. Place in a pot with the coarsely chopped vegetables, some salt, and herbs, cover with water and simmer gently (uncovered) until tender.

Remove the meat. Set the stock aside and season heartily with salt, pepper, a dash of vinegar and sugar to give a sweet-and-sour flavor. Return to heat and stir in 6 beaten egg whites. Boil very briefly and set aside to clear. Strain through a cheese-cloth.

Remove the goose meat from the bones and cut into generous slices. Place in glass molds and cover with the stock.

Serve with fried potatoes made from cold potatoes boiled in their jackets.

Black Jellied Goose

This is a typical Berlin specialty, served in every upper-class household before the war. Today it is in danger of being forgotten.

1200 grams goose with bones, 1 kilogram calves' feet, 150 grams root vegetables, 150 grams gingerbread, 100 grams pigs' blood, salt, pepper, vinegar, a dash of sugar.

Wash and clean the goose and calves' feet well. If necessary, divide the goose into large pieces.

Cover the goose and calves' feet with water and boil with the coarsely chopped vegetables (celery root, leek, carrots), salt and simmer slowly until tender.

Remove meat.

Bind the stock with the crushed gingerbread and stirred pigs' blood. Bring to a boil briefly and remove from heat. Season to taste with salt, pepper, sugar, and vinegar for a sweet-and-sour flavor. Set aside to cool.

Carefully remove the goose meat from the bones. Using a sharp knife, cut diagonally into large slices.

Place meat in molds and pour over the stock right before it thickens. Serve with fried potatoes made from potatoes boiled in their jackets.

Simple Herring Salad
as Still Served in Berlin Pubs

*4 salt or 8 matjes herring, 2 medium-sour apples,
2 kosher pickles, 1 large onion, 200 grams boiled
potatoes in their jackets, salt, pepper, vinegar, oil.*

Soak the herring as usual. Clean, and wash. Remove the milt and reserve.

Cut the herring fillets into small cubes. Pare and core the apples and dice, along with the pickles, onion, and cooled potatoes.

Mix the milt with some vinegar and oil and press through a sieve. Combine with the diced salad. If necessary, season with salt and pepper.

In Berlin this dish is accompanied by a slice of bread and butter or a roll.

In the traditional bistros of the last century such herring salad sat on the bar counter next to the potato salad, pickles, and meatballs, in brown earthenware dishes which widened at the top. Some may still remember these dishes; mothers and grandmothers used to use them for mixing cake dough.

If you would like to see what the forerunner of the cold buffet looked like, take a stroll through the "Berliner Weissbierstuben" in the Berlin Museum. You'll think you are right back in a bar in old Berlin.

Rollmops

*8 sour herring, ¼ liter milk for marinating, 1 table-
spoon mustard, 2 sour pickles, 1 tablespoon capers,
1 large onion, some toothpicks or wooden picks for
fastening.
For the cold sauce:
2 herring milts, 1 tablespoon mayonnaise, ½ cup
sweet cream, 4 peppercorns, 1 bay leaf, 1 sprig of
thyme, some basil and tarragon, salad oil.*

Clean and debone the herring. Cut off head. Soak in milk overnight. Remove from milk and spread the insides with mustard followed by layer of finely chopped onion, chopped capers, and a pickle slice approx. 5 cm long and as thick as a thumb. Roll the herring and fasten with a wooden pick so that it cannot open by itself.

Now mix the milt with mayonnaise. Stir in the cream, 1 tablespoon salad oil, and add the spices. Place the herring rolls in layers in a glass or porcelain jar and pour over the sauce.

Allow to steep for approx. 4 days. Serve with bread and butter, rolls, or plain, to get rid of a hangover.

Pickled Eggs

This is another typical beer snack that actually originated in Saxony where these eggs are still found on bar counters. They are refrigerated in covered glass jars similar to the early candy jars.

The tradition is preserved in the old Berlin "Weissbierstuben" of the Berlin Museum, located in the former Old Berlin Supreme Court. After a few too many rounds of beer and corn schnapps (a combination known as a "Gedecke") the bartender supplied one or two pickled eggs with mustard. And now for the recipe!

> *For the brine:*
> *1½ liters water, 150 grams salt, 2 bay leaves, 10 pimientos, 10 coriander seeds, 1 juniper berry, 16 grams dried dill.*
> *To boil the eggs:*
> *1 onion.*

Boil the water in a pot with the salt and spices. Allow to cool.

Boil 10 eggs with a peeled onion for 10 minutes. The onion will give the eggs a yellow tint.

Rinse eggs with cold water and crack each shell on the edge of the jar so the brine can penetrate.

Now place the eggs in the cooled brine and let steep for at least 24 hours. Serve with mustard or oil and vinegar mixed with finely chopped onions.

Pork Cutlets in Aspic with Fried Potatoes

4 pork cutlets, 2 calves' feet, 1 onion, 3 pimientos,
3 peppercorns, 1 bay leaf, 1 clove, 4 cornichons,
3 boiled eggs, 1 carrot, some capers, some tarragon
leaves, 2 egg whites, salt, pepper, 1–2 cups vinegar.

Split the calves' feet in half lengthwise. Together with the pork cutlets, boil in water briefly, then drain. Place in a pot with cold water, some salt, the onion, and the remaining spices and simmer for approx. 1 hour until tender. Remove pork cutlets and let calves' feet simmer gently for another 1½ hours. Strain the stock through a fine sieve and skim off the fat, first with a ladle, then with a clean paper towel.

Season the stock with salt, pepper, and vinegar. Using a whisk, beat the egg whites with a bit of water. Pour the egg whites into the hot stock and bring to a boil, stirring constantly. Remove from heat and cover. As soon as egg whites are firm and float to the surface, the jelly is clear, and you can strain the stock again. Pour the aspic into the bottom of the molds and after it hardens somewhat, add, as decoration, egg slices, cornichons cut lengthwise, and lightly boiled carrot slices together with capers and tarragon leaves. Then add the cutlets and pour the remaining aspic over them. Chill. You could also get by without molds by coating the cold pork cutlets with aspic, garnishing with the sliced vegetables, placing them in a baking pan and covering them with more (cold) aspic.

Cut the remaining chilled aspic into cubes for decoration. Serve the cutlets in aspic with fried potatoes.

Have a draft
beer with it.

Notes and more recipes

Sweets and Pastries

Semolina Porridge

For the porridge:
½ liter milk, 20 grams sugar, 1 package vanilla sugar,
45–50 grams semolina, a dash of salt, 2 egg yolks,
1 egg white.
For the sauce:
350 grams fresh fruits of the season, strawberries, cur-
rants, cranberries (or preserves), sugar, 1 tablespoon
cornstarch.

Bring to a boil milk, sugar, vanilla sugar, and salt. Gradually stir in semolina with a whisk. Take care that the porridge does not get too thick. Mix the egg yolks with a bit of milk and stir into porridge. Remove from heat. Now beat the egg white until stiff and stir into the porridge. Pour into bowls or molds.

If you use fresh fruit, wash well and cook in ¼ liter water until soft. Sweeten with some sugar and thicken with the cornstarch dissolved in water.

Pour the sauce over the porridge and serve.

Poppy Seed Trifle

It used to be customary in old Berlin to make poppy seed trifle around Christmas and New Year's. They were a favorite of young and old, served cold with grog to drink for the older generation. Try it. Maybe the custom can be revived.

3 stale rolls, 1 liter milk, 250 grams sugar, 250 grams
ground, dark poppy seeds, 60 grams raisins,
60 grams sweet almonds.

Slice the rolls into thumb-sized slices and place in a deep dish with ½ liter milk. Soak thoroughly and sprinkle with 50 grams sugar.

Cook the poppy seeds slowly with the remaining ½ liter milk, 200 grams sugar and the raisins for approx. 10 minutes.

Place the poppy seeds and bread in alternate layers in a glass bowl. Top with the sweet shredded or ground almonds.

Serve in portions on glass plates.

Rote Grütze

*300 grams raspberries, 300 grams currants, 150 grams
sugar, 100 grams cornstarch.
For the sauce:
¼ liter sweet cream, 10 grams sugar.*

Wash the raspberries and currants and cook until soft in ¾ liter
water. Put through a strainer and add the sugar.

Bring the fruit juice and sugar to a boil again, then add the
cornstach dissolved in ½ cup water. Stir in with a whisk and boil
briefly.

Pour the Grütze into bowls or molds and let cool.

Lightly beat the cream with a whisk to thicken somewhat, sweeten
with sugar and pour over the dessert.

Apple Fritters

This is a warm dessert that originated in Berlin and is especially popular during the colder months. In prewar Berlin it was commonly served in all upper-class households. It was even popular during Queen Luise's day.

4 large ripe apples, 30 grams sugar, 1 tablespoon rum.
For deep frying:
1½ pounds lard or clarified butter.
For the batter:
250 grams flour, some water, approx. 1 glass beer,
3 tablespoons olive oil, a dash of salt, 4 egg whites.

Pare and core the apples. Cut into 3 or 4 cm thick slices. Sprinkle with sugar and rum and steep for approx. 45 minutes.

It is best to prepare the batter the night before.

Sift the flour. Combine with some water and beer and stir into a thick batter. Add the salt, stir in the olive oil and finally fold in the stiff egg whites.

Dip the drained apples into the batter and deep fry in the hot fat until light brown. Remove and sprinkle with cinnamon sugar. Serve hot.

Banana, pineapple, and apricot fritters may be prepared in the same way.

Poor Knights

(French Toast)

4 slices slightly stale white bread, ¼ liter milk, some grated lemon peel, sugar, cinnamon, 4 whole eggs, 60–80 grams butter.

Boil the milk with the sugar, cinnamon, and grated lemon peel. Let cool.

Soak the bread thoroughly in the cooled milk. Then dip the bread in the beaten eggs and brown on both sides in a hot, buttered griddle.

Serve sprinkled with sugar.

It is also customary to serve with compote of seasonal fruit.

Heavenly . . .

Berliner Luft

This is a culinary reproduction of the popular song "Das ist die Berliner Luft, Luft Luft . . ."

It originated about the same time as Art Nouveau.

> *12 eggs (separated into yolks and whites, the egg whites must be free of any yolk), juice and peel of 1 lemon (unsprayed), 12 grams gelatine, approx. 90 grams sugar cubes.*
> *For the sauce:*
> *250 grams fresh, washed strawberries or other seasonal berry fruit, 50 grams superfine sugar.*

To prepare the sauce strain the strawberries and boil in a small amount of water with the superfine sugar. Cool and set aside.

Rub the sugar cubes on the lemon peel and heat together with the egg yolks and lemon juice. Mix with a whisk until thick and creamy. Remove from heat and set aside. Stir in the dissolved gelatine and beat until cool.

Using a completely grease-free whisk and mixing bowl, beat the egg whites until stiff and elastic.

Fold the stiff egg whites into the egg and lemon mixture. Pour into a small pound cake pan and put in the freezer overnight.

Turn out of the mold and serve on glass plates or dessert plates topped with the chilled sauce. Accompany with waffles or sweet biscuits.

Berliner Baumkuchen

Older Berliners will still remember the most renowned Baum-kuchen bakery "Jaedicke" on Kochstrasse, in the old newspaper quarter. This bakery was already remarkably famous for these cakes at the turn of the century. After the war they moved to the Tegernsee in Bavaria and continued the tradition there.

To make a real Baumkuchen in the shape of a tree-trunk, as the name implies, you would, of course, need the special baker's equipment. You can, however, make your own version by using the following recipe:

> *250 grams butter, 250 grams sugar, 2 teaspoons baking powder, 1 package vanilla sugar, 3 eggs and 3 egg yolks, 1 tablespoon rum, 185 grams cake flour, 70 grams cornstarch, 3 egg whites, butter to grease the pan, 200 grams confectioners' sugar and 3 spoonfuls water for the icing.*

Mix the butter, sugar, and vanilla sugar until creamy. Then gradu-ally stir in the egg yolks and whole eggs followed by the rum. Combine flour, cornstarch, and baking powder. Sift and stir into the foamy butter and egg mixture. Then fold in carefully the stiff egg whites. Grease a 25 or 30 centimeters diameter spring form pan with a bottom, and brush on a thin layer of the batter. Bake in the oven at moderate heat until the surface is golden. Then add the next layer, bake until golden and continue in this way until all the batter is used. Make the sugar icing and glaze the cooled cake with it.

Berlin Jelly Doughnuts

This Berlin specialty came about in the middle of the 18th century. On New Year's Eve especially it is consumed in massive amounts. The inventor is said to be a Berliner who drafted into the artillery, then deemed unfit, but kept on as the field baker instead. In gratitude therefore, it is said that he shaped his invention after the contemporary ammunition, i. e. round cannon balls.

116

For the batter:
500 grams flour, 30 grams yeast, zest from ½ lemon,
1 pinch of salt, 100 grams sugar, ¼ liter milk, 1 egg,
1 egg yolk, 60 grams butter.
For the filling:
Approx. 175 grams jelly of your choice.
For deep frying:
500 grams clarified butter.

Dissolve the yeast in the lukewarm milk.

Sift flour, sugar, and salt together. Pour in a bowl and make a well in which the dissolved yeast will be poured to work into the dough. Place butter flakes, lemon zest, and eggs around the edge. Cover and set in a warm place. Work into a dough, cover. Let rise, then punch down. Roll out to approx. 7 millimeters thickness and cut 7 centimeters diameter rounds. Place a small portion of jelly on each round. Brush the edges with water and cap with another round. Let rise.

After allowing the pancakes to rise, place right side up in the hot fat and deep fry on both sides until golden brown. Dust with cinnamon sugar or powdered sugar or glaze with a sugar glaze.

Butter Pretzels

This is yet another Berlin specialty. Its popularity spread all the way to Leipzig.

For the starter:
250 grams sifted flour, 25 grams butter, 7 grams salt,
1 tablespoon sugar, 1¼ deciliter water.
To fold in:
200 grams soft butter.
To sprinkle:
1 egg yolk, approx. 75 grams coarse sugar

Mix the 25 grams butter with the flour and form into a ring either on the table or in a bowl. Now add the salt and sugar to the water, pour into the flour and knead several minutes into a smooth dough. Wrap in a cloth and chill 1 hour in the refrigerator. Cut into the doughball crosswise from the top and roll out into a cross shape. Form the butter into a cube and place in the center of the dough. Then fold the corners of the cross towards the center over the butter. Roll carefully into a square then fold both ends towards the center over one another so that you have three layers.

This was the first "turn." Place in the refrigerator for another 20 minutes and repeat the process above for a total of 5 to 6 turns. Take care each time not to dust the roller with too much flour. Roll the dough to 3 millimeters thickness and cut into pencil-thick, 30 centimeters long strips. Brush these with egg yolk and sprinkle with coarse sugar. Twist each strip into a pretzel shape and place on a baking sheet rinsed with water. Bake at moderate heat for approx. 15 minutes.

Berlin Poundcake

This cake is undoubtedly one of the many legacies of the Huguenots. It also proves that they had more to their credit than the invention of "Berliner Weisse." These courageous and hard working people settled, by order of the King, in what is now Moabit. They called this area "terre maudit," meaning barren land. Over the years, "terre maudit" was Germanized into Moabit. Historically, the poundcake is a "common" version of a Savarin.

The old Huguenot recipe is as follows:

> *500 grams butter, 3 whole eggs, 3 egg yolks, 250 grams sugar, 125 grams currant, 125 grams sultana raisins, 50 grams shaved citron, 15 grams finely ground bitter almonds, 1 pinch of salt, 1 tablespoon vanilla sugar, some grated lemon rind, 1 pinch of mace, 3 tablespoons brandy, 45 grams yeast, 1/8 liter milk, 625 grams cake flour.*

Pour the flour into a bowl and make a well in the center. Dissolve the yeast in lukewarm milk, work into the flour and let rise. Beat the butter until foamy and add remaining ingredients. After allowing the yeast to rise knead all ingredients into a dough until it blisters. Pour into an earthenware pound cake pan and let rise again. Bake in a moderate oven for about 1 hour until lightly browned. Remove from pan and dust with confectioners' sugar.

The older generation will still remember seeing women with cloth-covered poundcake pans on rushing to their local bakers on Saturdays to have their cakes baked for a fee. What a wonderful poundcake aroma mother would then bring back into the house . . .

Eberswalder Spritzkuchen
(Choux Paste Rings)

For the choux paste:
¼ liter water, 60 grams butter, 150 grams flour, 30 grams cornstarch, 1 pinch of salt, 5 eggs, 1 tablespoon sugar, 1 level teaspoon baking powder.
For deep frying:
600 grams clarified butter.
For the glaze:
200 grams confectioners' sugar.

Bring water to a boil with the 60 grams butter, salt, and sugar. Sift the flour with the cornstarch, then add to the water and stir with a wooden spatula until a milky coating begins to form on the bottom of the pot. Remove from heat and beat in the eggs one by one with the spatula. Finally, stir in the baking powder.

Pour the batter into a zigzag pastry bag and pour in rings on a piece of wax paper. Slide off the wax paper into the hot fat and deep fry for 4 minutes on either side until golden. Make a glaze with the confectioners' sugar and approx. 3 tablespoons warm water and brush over the warm choux rings.

Cream Puffs

Cream Puffs with whipped cream have always been a favorite treat.

Whipped cream was invented in 1720 at the Castle of Chantilly. It was brought to Berlin by Noël, the court chef of Frederick the Great. Noël was born in 1726 and died in 1801.

Cream puffs with whipped cream were also a favorite of Queen Luise's children as they romped around their estate near Potsdam during the summer.

75 grams butter, ¼ liter water or milk, 125 grams sifted flour, 1 pinch of salt, some vanilla, some grated lemon rind, a dash of sugar, some baking powder for better color, 4–5 eggs.

Bring to a vigorous boil the water or milk, add the butter. Then add the flour, and stir with a wooden spatula until the paste no longer clings to the pan.

Stir in the eggs one by one. Stir the mixture until smooth after adding each egg. Together with the first egg add spices and baking powder.

In the days without pastry bags a spoon was used to place the batter on the baking sheet. Today we use zigzag pastry bags to form small mounds on the baking sheet which are then brushed with egg yolk and deep fried at moderate heat. After cooling, cut open and fill with vanilla flavored whipped cream and dust with confectioners' sugar.

Cinnamon Pretzels

A woman from Spandau called "Alte Rieke" (old Rieke) went down in history for the cinnamon pretzels she sold on the street.

375 grams sifted flour, 240 grams superfine sugar, 125 grams soft butter, 3 eggs, 3 grams good, ground cinnamon, 1 teaspoon baking powder, salt.

The dough is prepared as follows:

Mix in a bowl eggs, butter and sugar. Mix the baking powder and cinnamon with the flour. Add a pinch of salt. Combine beaten eggs, sugar, and butter with the flour mixture. Work into a dough.

Form pretzels and place these on a lightly greased baking sheet. Brush with a mixture of water and egg yolk and bake in a moderate oven until golden.

Berliner Schusterjungen

400 grams rye flour, 200 grams wheat flour, 35 grams crumbled yeast, ⅜ liter lukewarm water, ½ teaspoon salt, 1 pinch of sugar.

Combine the sifted flours in a bowl, then mix in the salt. Dissolve the yeast and sugar in the lukewarm water. Make a well in the center of the flour and stir in the yeast. Cover and let rise in a warm place until doubled in bulk. Then knead into a dough which comes away from the sides of the bowl. Cover and let rise again. Bake in a preheated, hot oven for 20 minutes. Roll in some rye flour and let cool.

Slice and spread with goose or pork lard and top with "Harzer" cheese. Also tastes good with Hackepeter and diced onions.

Mikey loves it!

121

fig . 11

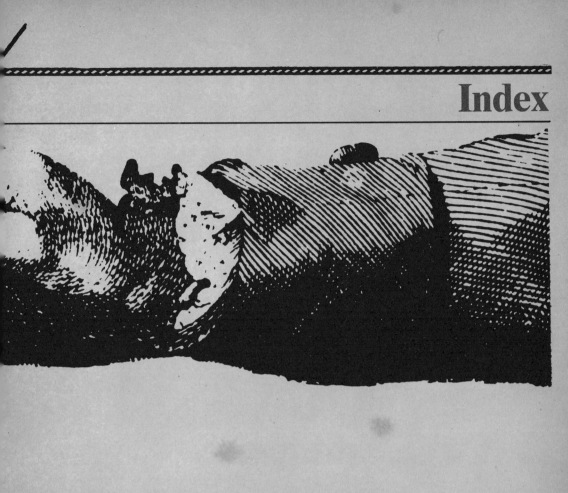

Index

Drinks

Ambrosia	30
Jenny Lind Punch	30
Kaiser Tea	31
Rose Wine	31
Waldmeister (Woodruff) Punch	32
Palace Punch	33

Soups

Cold Beer Soup	36
Barley Soup with Dried Prunes	36
Berlin Potato Soup	37
Crayfish Soup	37
Peas with Pork	38
Warm Beer Soup	39

Traditional, simple Dishes

Yeast Dumplings with Cooked Fruit	44
Boiled Potatoes with Farmers' Cheese and Linseed Oil	44
Schlesisches Himmelreich	45
Grandma's Berlin Kosher Pickles	46

Vegetables

Bouillon Potatoes	50
Berlin Potato Pancakes	50
Puréed Peas	51
Steamed Cucumbers	51
Leipziger Allerlei	52
Asparagus Spears	53
Asparagus Spears in Dill Cream Sauce	54
Teltower Turnips	54

Egg Dishes

Old Fashioned Bacon and Egg Pancakes with Salad   58
Hoppel-Poppel   58
Boiled Eggs with Mustard Sauce   59
Sour Eggs with Bacon Sauce   59

Fish Dishes

Fried Grass Pike   64
Pike in Spreewälder Sauce   64
Fried Pike with Potato Salad   65
Pike Dumplings   66
Sautéed Pike Perch with Potato Salad   66
Carp in Beer Sauce   67
Green Eel with Cucumber Salad and Buttered Potatoes   68
Crayfish in Dill Sauce   69
Poached Cod with Mustard Butter   69
Blue Tench   70
Tench in Dill Sauce   71

Meat and Poultry Dishes

Meat Patties   76
Pigs' Knuckles   76
Casseler Spare-Ribs   77
Meat Loaf with Cream Sauce   78
Ragout Fin   78
Fresh Blood Sausage and Liverwurst   79
Gänseklein with Parsley Sauce   80
Pickled Goose Legs   82
Roast Goose   82
Green Beans and Lamb   84
Berlin Chicken Fricassee   84
Berlin Zwiebelfleisch   86
Roasted Veal Brisket with Gooseberries   86
Berlin Veal Fricassee   87

Berlin Calf Liver   88
Stuffed Cabbage Rolls   88
Königsberger Klopse   89
Lung Hash with Fried Eggs   90
Pökelkamm   90
Braised Pig's Neck   91
Pork Belly   91
Stuffed Beef Rolls with Mashed Potatoes and Red Cabbage   92
Beef Brisket with Bouillon Potatoes,
Horseradish Sauce, and Red Beets   92
Prussian Tripe   93
Holstein Schnitzel   94
Stolzer Heinrich   96
Braised Rabbit Legs in Cream Sauce   96
The Hobby Gardener's Sunday Roast   97

Cold Dishes

Eel in Aspic   102
Bismarck Herring   102
Fried Herring   103
Hackepeter   104
White Jellied Goose   104
Black Jellied Goose   105
Simple Herring Salad as Still Served in Berlin Pubs   106
Rollmops   106
Pickled Eggs   107
Pork Cutlets in Aspic with Fried Potatoes   108

Sweets and Pastries

Semolina Porridge   112
Popply Seed Trifle   112
Rote Grütze   113
Apple Fritters   114
Poor Knights   114
Berliner Luft   115

Berliner Baumkuchen   116
Berlin Jelly Doughnuts   116
Butter Pretzels   117
Berlin Poundcake   118
Eberswalder Spritzkuchen   119
Cream Puffs   119
Cinnamon Pretzels   120
Berliner Schusterjungen   121

Metric Conversion Chart

	From:	Multiply By:	To Find:
fluid	milliliters	.034	fluid ounces
volume:	milliliters	.017	¼ cups
	milliliters	.004	cups
	milliliters	.001	fluid quarts
	liters	33.814	fluid ounces
	liters	4.22	cups
	liters	1.05	fluid quarts
mass/	grams	0.32	ounces
weight:	grams	.002	pounds
	kilograms	2.2	pounds
length:	millimeters	0.04	inches
	centimeters	0.4	inches
	meters	3.3	feet

We have also English language editions of the following titles.

Cooking in Vienna (forthcoming)